Praise for *Made Possible*

'*Made Possible* is a bold wake-up call for those who doubt what people with learning disabilities can do. Saba Salman's heart-lifting and truthful book is filled with extraordinary success stories (and also a smattering of comedy, swearing and sex) but doesn't shy away from the difficulties and challenges faced by people (like my son and her sister) who society calls 'different'. *Made Possible* suggests that everyone can live a successful, fulfilling life and asks that people with learning disabilities should not simply be tolerated, but wholeheartedly embraced and celebrated for their talents and potential.'

Sally Phillips, actor and writer

'The othering of people with learning disabilities has caused far too little concern. In *Made Possible*, actors, campaigners, songwriters, athletes, artists, filmmakers and politicians speak about what they have made of lives affected by a learning disability. This timely and essential collection gives their moving, varied and inspiring stories a valuable chance to breathe.'

Charles Fernyhough, writer, psychologist and editor of *Others*

'What a gem of an anthology that Saba Salman has compiled, providing a myriad of perspectives on people with learning disabilities, who are so rarely given a voice. This collection will educate and inspire in equal measure, and will contribute to our growing understanding, acceptance and celebration of "neurodiversity".'

niversity

'This is a wonderful book with an incredibly important message. It gives a voice to people with learning disability. Still too often treated as second-class citizens, with their human rights violated, Saba Salman demonstrates how people with learning disability can, with the right support and encouragement, be successful. This is a collection of life-affirming accounts of people realising their ambitions. But the challenge for all of us is that, for many other people with a learning disability, life is severely limited. Too many people remain in institutions. Outrageously, support for people living in the community has been trimmed back, leaving many people with the bare minimum support. Too often, the sort of things that make life worth living have been withdrawn. We deny people their right to flourish, to live life to the full. This book must act as a call to arms to confront continued discrimination. It shows what's possible. *Made Possible* must become the reality for all those with a learning disability.'

Sir Norman Lamb, chair of South London
and Maudsley NHS Foundation Trust, mental health and
learning disability campaigner and former health minister

'Saba and Raana's heart-warming book challenges and sustains in equal measure; it's about being human. I recognise so much of my son's life in the stories that Saba has gathered and so many of the experiences, both good and bad, that he has faced too. I recognise Saba's voice as a sister and know that Nigel's three sisters will laugh and cry through these tales too.

They will recognise the battles that my husband and I have faced with endless "so what?" reports about Nigel destined for inaction, with such low aspirations on the part of some of his teachers and assessors. But they will love the stories of triumph and the successes, because they also learnt early in life that success comes in different shapes and sizes.

A world in which people with learning disabilities are shut away is a diminished world, in which so called able-bodied people are the ones in straightjackets, quite unable to enjoy the creative ways that some of the people we read about in this book have brought new meaning and energy and love to life.

In my work and advocacy for my son and his friends and peers, I have learnt that there is "nothing about them without them". That everything is truly better when it is thought about, planned and executed together. That's why the wordless stories that Beyond Words has created over the last thirty years still owe their success to Nigel's inspiration and leadership. Saba and Raana have created a beautiful book and I applaud them.'

Baroness Sheila Hollins,
Independent life peer, emeritus professor in psychiatry of
learning disability, and founder of the charity Beyond Words

'You will never have read anything quite as authentic and truly inclusive, or encountered voices more vibrant and diverse. Saba Salman's excellent book shows us that a learning disability is no barrier to achieving your aspirations.'

Sir Richard Stilgoe, founder and trustee, The Orpheus Centre

'Saba Salman's book demonstrates how much society will lose without the active engagement of all of our citizens. As long as we treat people with learning difficulties as individuals to be pitied, overlooked and occasionally studied, we will never know just how much of a contribution they can make. Without a trace of sentimentality, or false heroism, Salman shows us that the obstacles many people face are not due to their own capabilities, but are caused by systems and structures that assume inadequacy and deficit, rather than contribution and value. None of us is independent. None of us has capability on every front. All of us need help to survive, and to thrive. This book reminds us of our common humanity, our shared desire to be part of something bigger than ourselves, and most importantly, how much we all lose by treating those with learning difficulties as lesser people than ourselves. Renewed and re-energised civil society needs the active engagement of all of our citizens. Without that we will never succeed.'

Dame Julia Unwin, chair,
Independent Inquiry on the Future of Civil Society

'Saba Salman's moving, funny and truthful book provides a wonderful opportunity to hear directly *from* people with learning disabilities, rather than just read about them. She clearly articulates, through her own family experience, the current challenging environment for people with different forms of disability, before bringing together an honest, vivid, moving and entertaining treasury of essays. There are moments of insight, humour and humanity in every story, and I will come back to this book again and again whenever I need to hear these magnificent people telling their truth.'

Michael Price,
Emmy Award-winning composer,
pianist and trustee, Heart n Soul

'Saba Salman has brought together a truly outstanding collection of essays. Each one challenges assumptions, asking us to think about issues facing the individual but also the wider implications for society. The openness and heartfelt nature of each story makes them even more powerful. This is a book for everyone; from policymakers to people at large. The fundamental message is that we can and *should* do better.'

Mark Malcolmson, principal and chief executive, City Lit

'This book deals an earth-shattering blow to every preconception about people with learning disabilities. A fantastic, nuanced read.'

Madani Younis, chief executive producer, The Shed, New York and former creative director, Southbank Centre

'This is exactly what we need. It is stories like these that break through the prejudice that stops so many people with learning disabilities from fulfilling their potential. It is stories like these that reveal our shared need for love, freedom and lives of citizenship. This book is a milestone in the ongoing battle for equal rights and inclusion.'

Dr Simon Duffy, founder and director,
Centre for Welfare Reform

'Saba Salman's brilliant book arrives just as we need it more than ever. A hugely enjoyable, enlightening and absolutely essential collection of essays.'

Ben Weatherill, playwright

'*Made Possible* features beautifully human stories of achievement from people in their own words, with warmth, humour, great insight and grit. Most powerful, though, is the fact that these are tales of ordinary lives told by people who all want to achieve good things for themselves, their family and their community. *Made Possible* is an intensely personal book and reminds us how people with learning disabilities are our friends, neighbours and fellow citizens – rather than just 'case studies' or 'clients', which is more commonly how we hear about the lives of learning-disabled people.'

Samantha Clark, chief executive, Learning Disability England

'I believe that we all have potential and we all shine in different ways, and this truth is laid bare in *Made Possible*. Normalising the conversation about difference starts with seeing the role models who are leading the way, like the people who share their success stories in this book. *Made Possible* is essential reading because when we engage, we learn and we break down barriers. This book shows us that everyone has the right to a successful and fulfilling life and the different ways that this can be achieved.'

Kamran Mallick, chief executive, Disability Rights UK

'The achievements of the collection of trailblazing writers featured are awe-inspiring stories of success by any standards. Their voices are a beacon, lighting the way for families like mine. Yet equally, it was the everyday achievements and the human connections that drew me in to *Made Possible* and kept me reading. Saba's depiction of her relationship with her sister Raana made me reflect on that between my own daughters: the pride and protectiveness, the deep love, the innovative ways to overcome challenges and the delicious moments of humour. This is what make our lives so rich.

A common thread running through the book is the writers' overwhelming desires to 'prove them wrong'. This is a slogan my daughter, who has Down's syndrome, proudly wears on a badge her sister bought her. It's this burning motivation that sets goals and sparks immense efforts to achieve greatness or what is sometimes considered by others to be ordinary and everyday.

My daughter may well grow up to excel in an arena that inspires others like her. Or she may not. She won't be "inspiring" just for leading her life her way with the right support, respect and the knowledge that she is appreciated for being exactly who she is. But, like everyone featured in the book, she will still be a success.'

Hayley Newman, author, speaker,
campaigner and founder of the Downs Side Up blog

'This book sets out the stories of eight people who've achieved success in diverse settings such as the performing arts, athletics, politics and campaigning. They happen to have a learning disability. Their accounts offer a beacon of hope and light in a dark world of repeated failures by the state to offer basic support and life opportunities to too many of their peers. This is a compelling and engaging read that should challenge our thinking and assumptions about how we can enable people to have a good life.'

Richard Humphries, senior fellow, The King's Fund

'I love reading about people who find their calling doing different things to me, how they go about it, and how they got to where they are, so *Made Possible* is right up my street. Eight very different people with very different lives, all grippingly told, and endlessly quotable. Can't wait to read it again.'

Chris Hatton, professor of public health
and disability, Lancaster University

MADE
POSSIBLE

Stories of success by people with learning disabilities –
in their own words

Edited by SABA SALMAN

unbound

First published in 2020

Unbound
6th Floor Mutual House, 70 Conduit Street, London W1S 2GF
www.unbound.com
All rights reserved

© Saba Salman, 2020
Individual work © respective contributors, 2020

Text design by PDQ Digital Media Solutions Ltd

A CIP record for this book is available from the British Library

ISBN 978-1-78352-825-7 (hardback)
ISBN 978-1-78352-826-4 (paperback)
ISBN 978-1-78352-827-1 (ebook)

Printed and bound in Great Britain by Clays Ltd, Elcograf S.p.A.

1 3 5 7 9 8 6 4 2

For – and because of – Raana

Contents

Editor's Note

The true origins of *Made Possible* lie in an event that took place around thirty years ago: the arrival of my youngest sister, Raana. The idea for a book based on her achievements came from seeing her grow up and become more independent. I wanted to write about my sister's potential and personality as a way to challenge society's negative attitudes towards learning-disabled people.

What turned this initial concept into the more tangible book you have in front of you now is the niggling feeling I was left with after writing an article about learning disability. I could see how my deadlines and word counts meant that people's stories simply didn't have room to breathe. Their experiences were dramatic, moving, compelling and entertaining – and I was cutting them short. I was also aware that much of what I was doing was using *my* words to write stories *about* people when in fact *their* stories, in *their own* words would be infinitely more powerful.

As for how the essay contributors were chosen, the fact is that I'm a journalist and this book simply wouldn't exist without my contacts book. I invited essays from people I was familiar with because I knew how engaging their stories were and I wanted more people to read them. I also approached those who could reflect different sorts of success in a range of professions. The contributors to this book are a diverse range of trailblazers who have excelled in competitive fields like film, theatre, music, art, campaigning, politics and sport. And the book focuses on adults who have a moderate learning disability because that's what my sister has, so that's what my family and I have experience of.[1]

When it came to writing the essays, the process was different for each individual. People had great stories to tell and just needed a hand with getting them down on paper. I supported each essayist as much or as little as they wanted. Generally though, we met, we talked, we Skyped, we emailed, we texted and we had many long telephone calls. Some people dictated all or part of their essay. Others prepared notes or had other material – like CVs or newspaper clippings – which they wanted to incorporate or expand on. A few were keen to use things they'd written in the past as a starting point. Many also had help from family, friends or colleagues with logistics (like arranging our editorial sessions or checking the dates and details included in their essays). But every single person had clear ideas about how their essay should look and feel; the tone, content and style are theirs, and theirs alone.[2]

I don't pretend that *Made Possible* is a comprehensive picture of learning disability and of all learning-disabled people – not least because there is no 'typical' person with a learning disability. Neither does this book offer an exhaustive history of learning disability, or indeed a detailed rundown of the contemporary socioeconomic landscape that affects people's lives today.

Instead, *Made Possible* will give you a glimpse of the many types of success that can be achieved by people with a learning disability – and what we as a society miss out on by overlooking them.

Saba Salman, 2020

Untold Success

Saba Salman

'What do you want to be when you grow up?' How often are we asked this question as children? How often do we ask this of children? The way we define and measure success might change as we grow older, but ideas about aspiration, accomplishments and potential are deeply ingrained from our childhood.

As young people we're ambitious about our education and job options. As adults we strive towards exciting social lives, fulfilling relationships, career promotions, salary rises and stimulating leisure interests. Once we're professionally established, we might share the secrets of our success, maybe inspire others to follow our paths, and we aim to have the perfect work/life balance. Growing older, we consider which achievements we're proudest of, whether that's owning our own homes, spending time with family and friends or having a stellar career.

And there's no end of ways to share our achievements, thanks to a multitude of social media platforms. There are visual squares of success on Instagram, posts about living the domestic dream on Facebook or announcements about work accolades on LinkedIn or Twitter.

A sense of purpose is what drives us – personally or professionally.

Success is a crucial part of being human.

But what if society didn't think success and aspiration applied to you?

My youngest sister, Raana, is among the 1.5 million people in the UK who have a learning disability, which broadly means that she finds it tricky to do some things independently and has trouble understanding other things unless they're simplified. When she was younger, she wouldn't have been asked, 'What do you want to be when you grow up?' As an adult, the question 'What do you do?' isn't one she's familiar with.

People with a learning disability aren't asked about what they want out of life. In fact, they aren't asked much at all and are rarely heard from first-hand. When's the last time you saw or heard someone with a learning disability on television, radio or in a newspaper or magazine? And while London hosting the 2012 Paralympics encouraged a shift in attitudes towards disability, the boost in awareness was short-lived (the focus was primarily on physical disability, although learning-disabled athletes competed in swimming, athletics and table tennis).

Usually, people like Raana are pitied as vulnerable victims, demonised as unproductive burdens on the state or patronised as inspirational figures who have triumphed over adversity. Success and ambition are human traits but are rarely associated with people like my sister. And if we fail to acknowledge the existence of these qualities in the lives of people with learning disabilities, we effectively treat them as less than human.

The essays in *Made Possible* focus mainly on career-related accomplishments because professional recognition is, in general, society's most common way of measuring people's achievements. But, thanks to my sister, I know that success can take many different forms.

Made Possible is also a timely book because it describes the support that people need to live fulfilling lives just as some of that support is shrinking. Government austerity in the UK from 2008 onwards has led to public-spending cuts at local councils that fund services like special needs education and social care.[3] One in four learning-disabled adults spends less than an hour outside their home every day as a result of the cuts, according to a study by learning disability charity Mencap.[4]

Susie, for example, has Down's syndrome and lives in the south of England. She used to have a one-to-one support worker for twelve hours a week that meant she had help with things like getting ready to go out or sorting out bills. But in 2010 Susie's support was cut to one two-hour visit a week, so she was mostly confined to her home apart from a weekly trip to the local library. As a result of her inactive lifestyle, Susie put on two stone in weight.[5]

Disabled people are disproportionately affected by government cuts. Research published in 2013 by the Centre for Welfare Reform about the impact of the cuts shows that people who aren't disabled or in poverty would lose £467 in income or services in a year, while the comparative figure for disabled people needing social care would be £8,832.[6]

What's more, the Conservative government's controversial welfare-reform programme has led to administrative chaos, a backlog in people's benefit payments and tighter eligibility criteria.

I helped fill out my sister's application for support when the welfare changes meant that one of her benefits (Disability Living Allowance) was replaced with another (Personal Independence Payments). The benefit is crucial because it helps her with day-to-day things like getting around. I'm used to wading through doorstep-thick reports full of social policy and government jargon, but dealing with this forty-page document required nerves of steel. The onerous, exhausting exercise involved repetitive requests for information about Raana's disability, forcing us to spell out what she needed help with several times over. It reduced her to nothing but a mass of inabilities.

Raana moved onto the new benefit, but welfare reforms mean that many people either get their support cut or lose it entirely.

One UN committee report concluded the UK government's austerity policies had resulted in 'grave or systematic violations' of disabled people's rights.[7] The reality of this, the UK's Equality and Human Rights Commission said, is that disabled people in general are treated like second-class citizens and people with learning disabilities are among those experiencing even greater barriers.[8] This is despite the fact that we have laws to promote and protect human rights and equality for all.

There's another reason that *Made Possible* is pertinent: the current assault on people's rights has led to a rise in grassroots activism and this book reflects the growth in campaigning across the learning disability movement. By taking control of the narrative in this book, its contributors reflect the growing sense of self-empowerment among people and families.

'Success,' as campaigner Shaun Webster explains in his essay on page 35, 'is about believing in yourself and making your own decisions.'

And that's where my sister's version of success comes in.

Everyday success

'I know you like that,' Raana announces, reaching under the Christmas tree and tapping a small, beautifully wrapped rectangular box.

It's 25 December 2005 and an ordinary family moment – the exchanging of gifts – is about to take on an extraordinary significance. Raana, sixteen years old, is back at my parents' house in West Sussex after her first term at a specialist residential college. She's just done her Christmas shopping independently for the first time (without her family but with her support workers), so I know she's hand-picked this present. I rip open the paper to reveal my favourite brand of peppermint tea. I well up immediately and give her an enormous hug. By the time Raana's handed out everyone's gifts, each thoughtfully chosen by *her* from *her* local shops, the room is a blur of tears and torn wrapping paper and my sister is beaming with pride.

Society would never regard Raana as successful. Dictionary definitions of the word 'successful' refer to accomplishing an aim or achieving fame, wealth or social status. Raana doesn't have a career like the essayists in *Made Possible* and she hasn't won any national plaudits for her skills. In fact, most people would consider what I've just described as unremarkable. Yet that Christmas was a landmark moment in Raana's own success story; her growing independence meant that she chose what to buy, where to buy it and that she paid for it all herself. This 'everyday success' is as significant as the grander ambitions described elsewhere in this book.

The fact is that until that Christmas, shopping was something Raana found traumatic because she's always disliked unfamiliar, noisy and crowded places and she finds money confusing to handle. If Raana felt uncomfortable in a shop, she'd sometimes shout, 'NO!' over and over again, and her frustration would escalate into what disapproving passers-by would assume to be a tantrum.

Raana's sensory sensitivity and anxiety is just one aspect of fragile X syndrome, the most common inherited cause of learning disability in the world. The genetic condition, which affects one in 4,000 males and one in 6,000 females,[9] is diagnosed by a blood test that identifies the 'fragile' site on the X chromosome. My mother is a carrier but is unaffected, and only the genetic lottery meant that she passed the syndrome to Raana, but not to me or my other sister, Abi. People with fragile X have mild to severe learning disabilities, although there's no 'typical' person with fragile X. The common characteristics can include social and emotional issues (anxiety, for example) as well as the kind of behaviour usually associated with autism, like obsessive tendencies.

I was seventeen years old when Raana was born and soon noticed how my sister was slower to walk, talk, read and write than her peers. Today, she still finds it hard to understand instructions or to concentrate; she has very little spatial awareness and finds hand-eye coordination difficult. She needs help with things like cutting her fingernails or crossing the road. She will need lifelong support.

For several months when Raana was younger, family excursions would involve packing a few small towels, just in case Raana got so stressed that she threw up.

The pile of fresh flannels that my mother stacked by the front door was a fluffy barometer of stress, simultaneously tragic and comic (the higher the pile, the greater the probability of vomiting). Raana preferred sticking to a familiar routine, so her stress would be triggered by anything from moving class to meeting new people.

When she was eleven, I remember a spell of skin picking, which reached its bloody peak during what was meant to be an overnight visit to my new flat in London. I'd explained what the place was like and what we'd be doing, and Raana was excited during the drive up from Sussex. But as soon as we arrived, she became increasingly distressed at the unfamiliar surroundings and started gouging her hands and arms with her fingernails. No amount of comfort, reassurance or distraction helped, so I drove her home, crying most of the way (Raana audibly, me internally). I felt I'd failed Raana as a sister and was desperately worried that her world was limited to school and home, and that this didn't bode well for her future.

That's why what Raana's achieved since those days – and what she continues to achieve – deserves recognition.

After college, she moved to a supported living scheme (housing combined with personal care) for learning-disabled people in Hampshire. Here, where she still lives, her achievements include helping to interview prospective housemates when a vacancy comes up in her shared house, learning to make everything from chocolate-chip biscuits to focaccia in the on-site bakery and going out to local pubs and restaurants or Zumba classes.

When Raana was twenty-one and had been in Hampshire just a few weeks, she took me to her local supermarket. I watched in awe as my once retail-phobic sister weaved through bodies and baskets to do her weekly shop. She queued patiently, confidently asked the cashier for some stamps and then announced she was paying by card (no need to handle those pesky notes and coins).

'I do shopping every Saturday,' Raana once said when I asked her about her weekend plans. 'Is anybody noticing? I just do it!'

So what's made my sister's success possible?

Firstly, my family has fought for Raana to have the right support. It's easy to assume that if your relative has a learning disability, 'the system' will step in to help you navigate your way towards the best help. But the reality is that you're jettisoned into the complicated, bewildering worlds of special needs education, health and social care.

You have to deal with a revolving door of professionals, including health visitors, GPs, paediatricians, special educational needs coordinators, social workers, care managers, speech and language therapists, occupational therapists and physiotherapists. As a result of this, my mother's developed the lobbying skills of a parliamentary campaigner, the negotiation expertise of a mediator and the single-minded determination of an army general.

My mother is not a woman to be messed with.

At Raana's mainstream primary school, we got her what was then known as a statement of special educational needs (these are now called education, health and care plans). This outlined the additional help she needed at school for what we then knew to be a moderate learning disability.

Although we didn't want to further label my sister – she's a person, not a condition – we knew that getting more information about Raana's specific support needs was important if she was to get the right help in the future. We got the diagnosis of fragile X when Raana was thirteen, by which time we'd successfully applied to the local education authority for a place at a mainstream secondary with a special needs unit. It wasn't the nearest one, but it had an excellent reputation for inclusive education.

By the time she left secondary school, we'd amassed a raft of professional reports on what support Raana needed (like one-to-one support in certain lessons), and this proved to be vital evidence in our application to her specialist college and beyond.

This potted history of getting Raana the right help belies the fact that it was often two steps forward, one step back. The process would suddenly be stalled because we'd be allocated a new social worker and have to explain the facts all over again, or we'd find that the perfect support existed, but it was too far away. It's also the case that not everyone has the time, energy and wherewithal to negotiate the support maze and fight for the best outcomes – be that for a child or an adult.

For anyone whose relative has profound and multiple learning disabilities (like a severe learning disability as well as a physical disability and a medical condition), the battle is even more arduous. This is because complex needs require high levels of support and these don't easily fit into the care services that exist. And crucially, the special educational needs landscape today is very different from what it was twenty years ago when we were looking for schools for Raana. Funding cuts are undermining the specialist educational support that is a fundamental building block if disabled children and young people are to go on and reach their potential.[10] Without access to the right help at school, a generation of children will be failed.

Raana's success is also down to the dedicated and enlightened individuals who have supported her over the years. She thrived at her secondary school, the Angmering School. She left with one GCSE (a grade C in art and design), a gold commendation award and a signed letter of achievement from the head teacher 'for setting such a positive example to other students'. She was prouder of the award and letter than the exam pass.

At her residential college, the Mount in East Sussex, she developed her reading, writing, numeracy and communication skills and enjoyed creative sessions in drama, art and gardening. At her current home, the Lantern Community in Hampshire, she's training as a baker. Both the Mount and the Lantern follow the ethos of the international Camphill Movement,[11] a core value of which is focusing on people's abilities, not their disabilities.

Of course, Raana's own determination, resilience and engaging personality have played a large part in her achievements. When her confidence grows – thanks to the right support – her personality shines.

In the best environment for her, Raana's a social person. She takes part in a neighbourhood carnival in Sussex every year, joining a float organised by Superstar Arts, a creative charity that does summer workshops.

Her resilience was clear when a much-loved uncle passed away. Raana's instinctive reaction was to tell us funny anecdotes about what he'd said or done, leading our grieving in a way that encouraged us to celebrate the man who'd lived, rather than simply focus on our loss.

For someone who doesn't like speaking on the phone, finds reading and writing a challenge and is usually monosyllabic, it's ironic that Raana's humour is often word-based. She loves making up nicknames and has declared that one of the minibuses at the Lantern is a female vehicle called 'Precious' (the name's been adopted by her housemates and support staff alike). One of her trademark lines when she wants to show her disapproval is 'You're fried!' – her take on Alan Sugar's catchphrase from television's *The Apprentice*. And, thanks to Raana's malapropism (she misheard a playground insult when she was younger), the phrase 'puck off' is our family's expletive of choice.

I asked her how she felt about influencing this book; 'proud' was her short answer.

Here's a characteristic exchange that hints at her sense of humour:

Me: What's the best thing about where you live?
Raana: I get to do things I enjoy like making stuff in pottery and baking, going out and eating out, also going to see shows. I enjoy washing Precious.
Me: How would you describe what you do?
Raana: I'm a baker!
Me: What do you like about baking?
Raana: Making the bread.
Me: What do you like best about making bread?
Raana: Eating it.

I love the fact that my sister has a busy life.
You've not replied to my texts, I messaged her recently.
Vey busy, came the typically misspelt reply.

Raana is sometimes too caught up in learning and socialising to contact us. And that can only be a good thing.

Different and therefore dangerous

Raana may be busy now, but had she been born fifty years earlier, her life would have been very different: my parents would have been advised by doctors to put her away in an institution and forget about her. That was standard medical advice in the 1960s.[12]

Today's negative perceptions of people with learning disabilities are a hangover from how they've been treated in the past.

In medieval England, for example, learning-disabled people were kept as court jesters or 'natural fools'[13] for entertainment. Some were cared for by their families or given shelter by monks or nuns. Others turned to begging, and the destitute ended up in the workhouses[14] that emerged in the eighteenth century. Given the lack of distinction back then between learning disability ('idiocy') and mental ill health ('lunacy'), the first facilities specifically for learning-disabled people ('asylums for idiots') didn't appear until the mid-nineteenth century. Entry was voluntary and the families of 'patients' paid towards their treatment, effectively restricting admission to those from wealthier backgrounds.

John Langdon Down was a pioneering doctor who opened one such establishment and identified the syndrome that eventually bore his name. The Normansfield Training Institution for Imbeciles opened in Teddington in 1868 as a private home for the 'care, education and treatment of those of good social position who present any degree of mental deficiency'.[15] It was a homely place, with residents encouraged to stroll in the tranquil gardens, share mealtimes with staff and learn 'life skills' like dressing or cooking. There was an ornate in-house theatre[16] and yearly trips to the Drury Lane Theatre in London. Places like Normansfield, however, were the exception, not the rule.

Institutions designed simply to warehouse the learning disabled mushroomed 'without restraint' in Victorian England, as the author Andy Merriman notes in *Tales of Normansfield: The Langdon Down Legacy*.[17] These were always in isolated locations, says Merriman, because people were regarded as 'different and therefore dangerous' and society 'had to be shielded from these "deviants"' – mental deficiency was synonymous with moral degeneracy.

Perceptions of the 'feeble-minded' as some sort of inferior species were encouraged by Darwin's theories on natural selection and the eugenics movement (later, of course, the Nazi regime regarded those with intellectual disabilities as 'useless eaters', subjecting them to compulsory sterilisation and involuntary euthanasia[18]).

Forcible segregation of people with learning disabilities began in the early twentieth century with the Mental Deficiency Act 1913, which allowed individuals to be transferred, without their consent, from workhouses to newly established 'mental deficiency colonies'.[19] By the 1950s, the NHS had become responsible for these soulless, badly staffed institutions that became known as long-stay hospitals.

> When I first went in there, even just getting out of the car you could hear the racket. You think you're going to a madhouse. When you first went there you could hear people screaming and shouting outside... The worst thing was, I couldn't wear my own clothes, you had to wear other people's... you just went to this big cupboard and helped yourself.

The late Mabel Cooper lived at St Lawrence's Hospital in Caterham, Surrey, for over twenty years. She went on to become a learning disability rights campaigner and shared her life story with the Open University's Social History of Learning Disability research group.[20]

A series of scandals from the 1960s onwards uncovered the appalling conditions in such long-stay hospitals and led to demands for them to close. These included mistreatment at Ely Hospital, Cardiff,[21] uncovered by the *News of the World* in 1967, and the harrowing 1981 documentary *Silent Minority*,[22] featuring scenes of a young man tied to a post in a long-stay hospital. There was even an inquiry into poor standards of care at the once visionary Normansfield.[23] Such cases led the government to publish the country's first-ever national policy on learning disability in a white paper in 1971.[24] There were recommendations to shut the institutions and create more housing and care in local communities.

But change was slow. In 1983, Susannah Seyman from the charity Down's Syndrome Association wrote about a disturbing visit to Normansfield, where she was first hit by the smell ('boiled cabbage, disinfectant and urine') and then shocked to see some of the residents naked. When Seyman asked why they weren't dressed, she was told 'they ruin their clothes when they wear them' and was then instructed to 'just step over' a naked woman lying on the ground. 'There was a sense of being in a kind of underworld where rules and expectations were a million miles away from what was acceptable at the time,' she wrote.[25]

In the book *First and Last: Closing Learning Disability Hospitals*,[26] Mark Brend recalled his experience as a support worker helping to move people from institutions into 'community settings' in the late 1980s. He collected two men from St Lawrence's in Surrey, each clutching a small black bin bag of old clothes made from 'an odd, quick-drying, shiny man-made fabric'. Neither had any personal mementoes with which to make a home, nor any job or friends to root them in their new neighbourhood.

Brend wrote, 'Almost uniquely, they were categorised as a sub-group amongst British citizens that had not committed crimes, and kept apart from mainstream life for most of their lives, then moved somewhere else without any say in the matter.'

The publication of the government's second national policy on learning disability came in a white paper in 2001.[27] Ambitiously titled *Valuing People*, it gave hope of better treatment. But just ten years later, in 2011, there was a horrible echo of past scandals when a BBC *Panorama* investigation exposed the systematic abuse of people with learning disabilities at the Winterbourne View hospital in South Gloucestershire, an NHS-funded private 'assessment and treatment unit'. Shocking undercover footage included staff dragging, slapping and brutally restraining the people they were meant to be helping. And for this 'care', the state was paying an average £3,500 per person per week. Margaret Flynn, author of the serious case review (an inquiry commissioned by a local council after allegations of abuse or neglect) of the hospital, said:

> We have been here before. There is nothing new about the institutional abuse of adults with learning disabilities and autism. Events witnessed at Winterbourne View hospital recall the custodial treatment associated with decommissioned, long-stay NHS hospitals.[28]

In theory, today's specialist secure units are designed to assess people with learning disabilities who also have mental health problems or whose 'behaviour presents a significant challenge to services'[29] (like self-harm). People are meant to stay only for a short time before they move back to their homes. In reality, people languish in these places for years, miles away from their families (the average stay at Winterbourne View was nineteen months, but some people had been there for more than three years).

Kept in seclusion, physically restrained or overmedicated to keep them quiet, it's little wonder that people's complex needs – the reason they're admitted to these units in the first place – simply escalate.

'I was put under heavy medication. I was out of it,' former local politician – and in his younger years a specialist-unit inpatient – Gavin Harding writes in his essay on page 183. 'Staff talked about me like I didn't exist. I felt invisible. How does anyone expect you to get better when you're treated like that?'

What happened at Winterbourne View was regarded at the time as a turning point in the treatment of people with learning disabilities: lessons would be learned, the government promised. The hospital closed, six staff were jailed and the government said it would move everyone – an estimated 3,500 people – from such units and into homes in local communities by 2014.[30]

But the deadline was missed.

At the end of October 2019, almost 2,200 people with learning disabilities and autism were still living in these unsuitable, inhumane, modern-day institutions.[31] Meanwhile, those who've been discharged from such places remain deeply scarred. Simon Tovey was abused at Winterbourne View, where staff kicked and punched him, and threatened to put his head down the toilet. Although Tovey eventually moved into his own home with support from carers, he faced an uphill struggle to recover from what he'd experienced. His mother Ann Earley said:

The Simon that returned to us was not the same one who left. He was profoundly affected and unable to put into words how he felt. He has a long-term fear of toilets – that's just one small thing. The other impact is incalculable, like his fear about what's going to happen next.[32]

The Victorian asylums have closed and the last long-stay NHS hospital shut in 2009, but as Winterbourne View and other abuse cases[33] since then have proved, their restrictive, institutional approach lingers. In late 2019, the government appointed crossbench life peer Baroness Sheila Hollins to chair an independent panel to review cases of those in long-term segregation. So-called 'locked rehabilitation wards'[34] are horribly reminiscent of long-stay institutions that are meant to have been consigned to history.[35] It's shocking that in modern Britain, a seventeen-year-old girl with a learning disability can be locked up in solitary confinement in a padded hospital room and fed through a hatch in the door.[36]

Every day, 30,000 to 35,000 adults with a learning disability are chemically restrained with psychotropic drugs even though they don't have the health conditions that these medicines are usually prescribed for.[37] Others are physically restrained[38] in hospital units like Winterbourne. One in three young adults spend less than an hour a day outside their homes,[39] and most residents living in supported housing are ready for bed at 8.30 p.m.[40]

But there are more serious risks than boredom and early bedtimes. Treating people with learning disabilities as second-class citizens puts their lives at stake. Numerous studies have shown that if you have a learning disability, you're more likely to die younger than everyone else because of poor care or delayed treatment.

One study commissioned by the NHS found that 28 per cent of people with learning disabilities die before they reach fifty, compared with 5 per cent of the general population.[41] In the UK you can expect to live till about eighty-four, but if you have a learning disability, according to the report, your life expectancy is around fifty-eight. Following the report, the government launched plans for better learning disability training for health and care staff – an issue that family campaigners had already been calling for.[42]

There have been growing demands in recent years for professionals to fully include families in the care of their learning-disabled relatives. The government report into the abuse at Winterbourne View, for example, found that staff didn't involve relatives in making decisions about their treatment or even allow them into the wards or bedrooms. In cases since Winterbourne View, people have died while being looked after by health or social care services and, after their death, it's frequently emerged that staff didn't properly communicate with families.[43]

There are cases of people dying unexpectedly while in state care, and their bereaved families have been forced to campaign to find out why, while also raising money for legal representation at inquests or having to represent themselves (you can't usually get legal aid for inquests). And all of this while still grieving.

This was the unimaginable horror experienced by Sara Ryan and her family when her eighteen-year-old son, Connor Sparrowhawk, died in 2013. Connor, also known as Laughing Boy, or LB, was a cool, stylish teenager who lived with his family in Oxford. He had a sharp sense of humour, a passion for lorries and buses, and he idolised David Bowie.

In March 2013, Connor, who had a learning disability, autism and epilepsy, became anxious and unpredictable and his family wasn't sure how to cope. They thought that an assessment at Slade House, a specialist unit run by Southern Health NHS Foundation Trust, would help get the right support.

But Connor never came out of the assessment and treatment centre; on 4 July 2013, he was found unconscious in the bath and died. He'd had an epileptic fit and drowned.

At first, the trust attributed his death to natural causes, but the family demanded an independent investigation, which concluded that Connor's death was preventable. Later, an inquest jury concluded that serious failings and neglect had contributed. Eventually Southern Health accepted responsibility for Connor's death.

None of this would have happened had it not been for the grassroots, family-led campaign Justice for LB (#JusticeforLB on social media). The breathtaking movement for change demanded not only the truth about how and why Connor died, but also equal rights and treatment for all learning-disabled people. The campaigners included people with learning disabilities, their families, professionals who worked in health and care, and university academics. Without the relentless pressure the NHS wouldn't have commissioned the wider inquiry into Southern Health that revealed that the trust had failed to investigate the deaths of 1,000 patients with learning disabilities or mental health issues. The inquiry showed that less than 1 per cent of unexpected deaths of people with learning disabilities were investigated.

By sharing images and stories of a much-loved son, brother, nephew and friend, campaigners ensured also that Connor wasn't simply another statistic in a news story, but a person with character and possibilities. This was a concerted effort by Sara Ryan and her husband Richard Huggins, Connor's stepfather, because they were frustrated at how media coverage of their experience negated their son's potential. Ryan wrote, 'He didn't have an imagined future, unlike news reports about other young people who die unexpectedly.'[44] In her book *Justice for Laughing Boy*, Ryan explains that Connor had ambitions to own a haulage company and marry 'a beautiful, brown-eyed woman', but the support staff involved in his care attached no importance to his aspirations.[45]

Today, Ryan still has huge concerns about the attitudes that exist in some parts of the health and care system. As Ryan told me when we met to talk about this anthology:

We shouldn't have to be climbing mountains for learning-disabled people to have the same rights as everybody else and to flourish. The problem isn't the general public's attitudes, because on the whole once people are 'comfortable' with difference they're absolutely fine. It's attitudes in the health and social care system that are the problem. Some professionals get sucked into historic perceptions that some people are less than human and lose their perspective because they're part of the system. But when people do get the fact that everyone has the right to have a good life, it creates joyousness because it brings everybody together and it makes for a much better society.

'Shhhhhh!'

Creating a better society for people with learning disabilities means a transformation of public attitudes alongside an improvement to the health and social care they receive.

As Laura Broughton explains in her essay on page 139, 'society treats you a little bit like a child' if you have a learning disability. And, as research proves, the reality is that the majority of people feel uncomfortable sitting next to someone like Raana in the cinema, or during a show.[46]

It was on a Saturday night in a theatre in London's West End that my sister and I experienced just how uncomfortable people can get about people with learning disabilities. I'd taken Raana to see her favourite show, *Grease the Musical*. She'd seen it before, but her familiarity with the lyrics and dance sequences only added to her enjoyment.

Raana doesn't like crowds, but she was so excited she shot determinedly through Piccadilly, wielding her rolled-up souvenir programme from a previous show like a crowd-dispersal baton, muttering, 'Out the way!' to nobody in particular.

As the curtain rose, she began slapping her thigh in

time to the music, clapping, whooping and singing (word perfect). She was so happy that at one point she stood up, legs spread wide, arms outstretched and – inspired by the moves to the song 'Greased Lightning' – swept one index finger across the horizon, left to right. Unfortunately, her enthusiasm didn't go down well with the people sitting in front of us, several of whom began staring, shooting us irritated glances and tutting. Finally, two women turned round, hissed a vitriolic, 'Shhhhhh!' and gestured angrily for my sister to sit down.

Raana looked confused.

'What exactly would you like me to do?' I fired back through clenched teeth.

Before the women could reply, an older lady next to me put her hand on mine and whispered calmly (but loudly enough for my sister's detractors to hear), 'She's special, let her be.'

She said Raana was only doing what others would if they weren't so 'uptight', and added that she had a granddaughter with Asperger syndrome. She was, mercifully, part of the 30 per cent of people who *do* feel comfortable sitting next to someone with a learning disability. Raana happily finger-clicked and toe-tapped her way through the remaining numbers.

Our brush with intolerant attitudes is nothing, though, compared to the experience of Mark Brookes. Brookes, who is in his fifties and lives in a flat in Essex, has been at the receiving end of bullying and hate crime since his twenties. Over the years, he's had everything from name-calling to being pelted with eggs and rotten fruit, which he told me about when we met to discuss *Made Possible*.

> I was walking down the street on my way home and I
> heard a car rev up behind me and a guy began calling
> me names like 'idiot' and 'mong'. The next thing I
> knew, someone had thrown something at me. Luckily
> it was only an egg and not a stone.

While Brookes reports incidents to the police, catching
the perpetrators is hard if he hasn't seen them and there
aren't any witnesses. His experience has led him to
become an anti-hate-crime campaigner, and he works
as an adviser on such issues with Dimensions, a not-
for-profit provider of support for adults with learning
disabilities and autism. His campaigning work earned
him an MBE in 2020.

According to a survey by Brookes' employer, 73 per
cent of people with learning disabilities or autism have
experienced hate crime,[47] and that can include anything
from cyberbullying to verbal and physical abuse (singer
Lizzie Emeh describes her unpleasant experiences of hate
crime in her essay on page 97).

Education, says Mark Brookes, will help tackle the issue:
'A lot of people still don't know what a learning disability
is, so it's about raising awareness among the public and
police, and encouraging people to report hate crime when
it happens.' Brookes believes that if people with learning
disabilities have 'a life in the community, jobs within their
community' it would have a positive impact on incidents

like the ones he's experienced. Referring to his own work, he adds, 'I do think of myself as successful. I'm definitely more confident because of it.'

Having hidden people with learning disabilities away for so long, it's no wonder that most of us are at best uncomfortable and at worst hostile when we see them.

It's a vicious circle of our own making.

'Come in … see what we do'

One reason that people like my sister are relatively invisible in society is that barely any of them have jobs.

Less than 6 per cent of people with learning disabilities work (and this figure has fallen over recent years[48]) but 65 per cent[49] actually want to work. Successive welfare-to-work schemes haven't really helped people with learning disabilities[50] or been specifically aimed at them.[51] Meanwhile, thanks to the public-sector spending cuts there are fewer council-funded supported employment projects to help learning-disabled people into work.[52]

Equality laws oblige employers to make reasonable adjustments to support disabled employees, like making application forms more accessible. But the fact is that most people don't associate learning-disabled people with job prospects; in a poll of a hundred MPs, 60 per cent said they didn't think people with learning disabilities could be supported into work.[53]

Michael Edwards is the founder and president of a charity that disproves this assumption. Edwards, who has a learning disability and is partially sighted, launched My

Life My Choice (MLMC) in Oxford twenty years ago. Today the award-winning organisation has more than forty people with learning disabilities on its books. Supported by colleagues without disabilities, they lead and deliver training courses on learning disability, act as consultants, and inspect services for organisations including the NHS, councils and police.

The charity is a user-led self-advocacy organisation, which means it's run by the kind of people it helps and it encourages others to speak up for themselves. Amongst other things, MLMC runs a travel training scheme (designed to help learning-disabled people travel safely and independently), a club night and a network of self-help groups that advise on anything from making friends to staying safe online.

Edwards launched MLMC after growing frustrated with the lack of opportunities open to people like him. He quit the council-run day centre he attended as a young man after discovering that staff were mixing up the plastic components he'd spent the entire morning sorting, just so he'd have a job to do in the afternoon.

I met with Edwards and some of his colleagues in Oxford in the summer of 2018 when I was doing research for this book, to learn more about the great work they do.

Edwards says, 'I think of myself as successful because I started something that's still going after almost twenty years and hopefully it'll carry on for a long time to come.'

Pam Bebbington, a freelance consultant at MLMC, lived in a long-stay hospital when she was younger. She says her work gives her purpose and is at odds with the negative connotations attached to learning disability. 'When you hear the words "learning disability" in the news it's usually about people being bullied or abused; that's the thing we hear all the time – or people neglecting them in hospital.' What does she think would make the biggest difference to the lives of people with learning disabilities? She says, without hesitation, 'The attitudes need to change.'

Paul Scarrott, vice chair of MLMC's board of trustees, who has spent time in an assessment and treatment unit, adds that he knows how to shift perceptions: 'People should come in and see our charity and see what we do – it would change people's minds.'

Scarrott's right. We need more recognition that learning-disabled people not only work, but that they can do more than simply collect supermarket trolleys or stack shelves. They can also run organisations themselves, supported by people without disabilities.

Gary Bourlet, for example, co-founded the national rights-based charity Learning Disability England. People should have not just a job but also a career, as he argues in his essay on page 75: 'Not everyone with a learning disability wants to work in a supermarket, but jobs for learning-disabled people aren't ever talked about in terms of professions. If they were, it could change how everyone sees us.'

There are many organisations blazing a trail for the employment of people with learning disabilities. When it launched in 1995, for example, Bristol-based cleaning firm A Clean Sweep became the first company in the UK to be run by people with learning disabilities. In Lancashire, Jen Blackwell, who has Down's syndrome, launched her own arts organisation, DanceSyndrome. London's Access All Areas is a theatre company of learning-disabled artists, all of whom are paid, and are supported by non-disabled staff. And there are charities employing the kind of people they usually support in admin or advisory roles, as hate-crime campaigner Mark Brookes proves.

There is also evidence to suggest that self-employment could be an option for getting more learning-disabled people into paid work,[54] even those with profound or multiple learning disabilities.

Delroy, a man with severe learning disabilities from Bristol, started a small business collecting and recycling plastic bottles in his neighbourhood with the help of support workers. Staff at the support charity Brandon Trust noticed how he liked to collect and crush plastic bottles at his care home before recycling them. Delroy's story was featured in a government report on employment[55] as an example of what could be done if people think creatively.

The late Jim Mansell, the influential professor of learning disability, believed that some form of work was possible for people with the most profound disabilities. In his study *Raising Our Sights*[56] Mansell described how work encourages social contact, leads to goals 'instead of purposelessness' and generates an income. Mansell acknowledged, however, that work would probably be among a range of activities for adults with profound and multiple disabilities, due to their complex needs. He added, 'The goal is that people should have the opportunity to take part in meaningful activities outside the home, including work, education and leisure.'

Mansell was challenging the status quo by arguing that success and aspiration should apply to everyone – even the most disabled, least visible people in society.

Refocusing

'Who's helped *you* to be here today?' the champion swimmer Dan Pepper asked me during an early conversation about his involvement in *Made Possible*. 'My family,' I said, explaining that 200 miles away from our meeting in Stockport, my mother was at my place, looking after my kids. 'Same here,' he nodded, adding that no one really acknowledges that all of us – whether or not we have a learning disability – need support of some kind. It's just the amount that varies (you can read his story on page 117).

When my parents are no longer here, Raana will still have the unequivocal support of her two sisters. But this isn't the case for those who either don't have siblings or other relatives, or whose family members aren't able to fight their corner. It's a well-documented fact that the biggest concern for parents of people with learning disabilities is not knowing what will happen to their son or daughter, and who will care for them, after they die.[57]

When I started working on this book, I had an email from an acquaintance whose brother has a learning disability. She explained that she'd heard about *Made Possible* and it had made her think of her role in helping her brother live a successful life. She preferred not to be named but shared her concerns:

My brother's care provider, the local authority and I were discussing my brother's sleeping issues and the social worker suggested sedating him! Thankfully, the care provider and I were equally stunned, and went on to have a more intelligent discussion about what was causing the sleep issues rather than loading him with sedatives – but it made me wonder about people that don't have a sister or family member to advocate for them.

Families of learning-disabled people are fundamental not only to helping people reach their goals, but to ensuring that their everyday care and support is the best it can possibly be.

Thanks mainly to the work of families and campaigners pushing for change, society today is generally a far better place for people with learning disabilities than it once was. The essays in *Made Possible* prove how people's potential can be realised and how they can lead not just ordinary and fulfilling lives, but extraordinarily impressive ones.

Yet it's almost fifty years ago since the UK first set out a more inclusive approach to people with learning disabilities in a white paper – we should have made much more progress since then.

The reams of evidence about the inequality experienced by learning-disabled people from birth to death are a sobering reminder of the disparity that still exists. There's also a risk that whatever progress has been made will be eroded by cuts to support that mean the difference between someone leaving their house or not.

Widespread and lasting change is harder to achieve when

there have only ever been two government white papers outlining a national policy on learning disability – and the most recent one of those, *Valuing People*, was almost twenty years ago. While *Valuing People* is still official policy, there's no drive to implement it and therefore no pressure to look comprehensively at learning-disabled people's access to housing, health, education and the community. There is nothing to force learning disability to the top of the national agenda.[58]

Rob Greig worked on delivering the changes outlined in the 2001 *Valuing People* policy as the government's then national director for learning disabilities. Just six years after the policy had launched, a senior Whitehall official told Greig that the issue had effectively had its brief spell in the spotlight and 'it's time for something else to be the focus'. Greig noted that it was 'a bit of a bizarre concept' that centuries of societal discrimination could be reversed in six years.[59]

The rights of learning-disabled people should be part of our national consciousness just like comparable equality debates on gender, race and sexuality.

There's a role for the media in influencing perceptions, from getting rid of descriptions of individuals as 'vulnerable' to including people with learning disabilities in print or broadcast news.

On stage and screen too, more authentic representations would mean that someone like my sister would find characters to identify with and see herself mirrored in. 'Drama,' argues actor Sarah Gordy in her essay on page 55, 'has to reflect the world as it is.' And filmmaker Matthew Hellett writes scathingly about 'awful stereotypes' in film and on television in his essay on page 161.

Success is something we all aspire to and we all have help to achieve, regardless of our abilities. What that success looks like depends on the individual. It may involve you winning a gong, being recognised nationally for your achievement or simply doing your own shopping. Success is a universal concept; there needs to be far greater acknowledgement that it applies to everyone, and that it can take many different forms.

People with learning disabilities are achieving all sorts of great things every day.

I'll leave the last word on that to my sister, Raana: 'Is anybody noticing?'

Saba Salman is a journalist, editor and regular writer on social affairs for the *Guardian*. She trained as a news reporter on London local papers before moving on to the nationals and becoming a correspondent for the *Evening Standard*. Saba's writing has featured in women's magazines as well as in specialist weekly titles on welfare, housing and local government.

Saba's journalism focuses on equality and disability issues and in particular the UK's overlooked population of 1.5 million people with learning disabilities. Saba is a fellow of the Royal Society of Arts and a trustee of the charity Sibs, which supports the siblings of disabled children and adults.

@Saba_Salman

Father Shaun

Shaun Webster, MBE

I am standing on my dad's doorstep. It's twenty years since he called me a retard. I haven't seen much of him since then. He told me I'd never work, never live on my own, never have a relationship. I'm here today, holding the MBE I was awarded for services to people with learning disabilities. I came on the bus from the flat where I live alone. I've got an ex-girlfriend standing next to me for moral support. I haven't told my dad I'm coming.

He opens the door. He smells of booze. He looks at me, confused.

'All right, Dad? You still a pisshead?'

'You can't talk to me like that!' he says.

'Why not?' I say. 'You've said so much bad stuff to me. You told me I'd never have a job, never live on my own. I've been abroad, Dad. I've met Prince Charles. He gave me this MBE.' I hold up the medal.

He's gobsmacked. I feel proud that I proved him wrong.

I've been wanting this day for years. It's not revenge – it's to prove who I am now.

My dad pushed me to push myself to prove him wrong. His words drove me to get where I am now, like an engine. He said to me I'd never have a job, never have kids and never do anything. He said I was too dumb. My dad was embarrassed about my learning disability and embarrassed that I went to a special school. I believed what he said for years.

In the past, I used to be ashamed of my learning disability because my dad used to put me down, especially after he'd been drinking. In the past I used to despise having a learning disability. I used to feel embarrassed, like a second-class citizen. But not now. I'm proud of my learning disability because I feel like I'm breaking down barriers as a human rights speaker and campaigner, which is what I got my MBE for.

I travel the world through my job as an international project worker at CHANGE, which is a human rights charity. My main job is to train organisations on how to make information accessible for people with learning disabilities and encourage them to support people better by actually listening to what they want. I feel that I'm changing attitudes and making a difference. I've got everything I wanted in life – kids, grandkids, work, a home – and I got it myself. It wasn't easy, but I got there.

My learning disability is a bit of me, but it's not a big deal and it doesn't define me. It hasn't stopped me having a life.

*

Success for me is about believing in yourself and making your own decisions. Success is about earning your own money and living independently. You can't have one without the other. Being employed gives you power, and having a role and responsibility makes you more independent. And when people are employed and live on their own, they can inspire others. The money I earn gives me opportunities to do things I always wanted to do – live in my own place, go to the pub, go shopping, go to the cinema.

I knew I didn't want to live with my mum till I was thirty or forty. So I put my name down for a council flat when I was sixteen years old. I moved out at twenty-one into a council flat in Rotherham, South Yorkshire, with my younger brother.

My mum had split up with my dad by then – she's an amazing woman; we have a brilliant relationship – and she also wanted me to be able to live on my own. The flat was close to my mum's, and my brother supported me with things like reading letters and cooking, but I felt I wasn't getting the chance to try things on my own. I love my brother and he wasn't doing anything bad; he just thought I'd struggle, so he did things for me. But I wanted to do everything like everyone else did – I wanted to cook, clean, dust, pay my bills – just like a normal person.

So I moved out on my own and I had help from a housing support organisation called KeyRing that helps people to live independently. The stepping stone to self-belief for me was when I got my own place. I got help from KeyRing with answering letters, dealing with bills, making appointments, that sort of thing. I had a fantastic support worker who did an action plan for me about things I wanted help with and I learned to do things on my own.

Shaun's signature Sunday bake

I can cook but I'm no chef – I get by. I didn't get the MBE for cooking, put it that way. But this is one of my favourite dishes – it really fills you up. Cook it on a Sunday and it could last into the week.

Ingredients

Four large potatoes, sliced or diced and cooked (part-boiled)
Half a block of grated cheese of your choice (I like to use Cheddar)
Two large uncooked handfuls of whatever filling you fancy (I like to use diced bacon or sliced sausages)

Method

Turn the oven to 200°C/400°F/Gas Mark 6. Grease a large baking tin with butter or oil. Put a layer of potato in the bottom of the tin. Cover with a layer of cheese, and then add the filling on top (this will be the middle of the bake). Then add another layer of potato and top this with a final layer of cheese. Bake for an hour or until browned and bubbling.

Serving suggestion

Serve with a large, lovely salad.

*

When I got my own place, one thing I wanted was to be more confident using public transport and to do my own shopping. Over time I became more confident in doing stuff for myself. Then I began to support other people with learning disabilities who KeyRing was helping to live on their own. What's great about how they help is that you're supported on your own terms. When you need support, you ask for it, and when you don't need it, you don't ask. It means you take charge of your life and make your own decisions. I don't need much support from KeyRing myself now, but I help other people who the charity supports.

Living on your own means you get freedom to go out and go back home any time you want. No one can tell you what to do. I can have my friends round to see me for drinks and anything else I want. I don't need to ask anyone if this is OK. My friends come round on a Friday night – we have beers, talk about politics, watch a movie. We might get a takeaway, get merry and wind each other up. They call me granddad, but I take the mick back. 'Steve, your hair's looking a bit thin these days!' I'll say to one of my mates. One of my friends has a learning disability, one hasn't, but we get on because we like the same things; we're just regular friends.

I like to go to the pub. I love going to the cinema. I like to watch sci-fi, horror, fantasy, true life and comedies. Sometimes I go to the cinema after work. I write movie reviews in my spare time and post them on Facebook. Sometimes I go to the cinema on my own and sometimes I go with my friends and make a night of it. I have the freedom to see any film I want, any time I want. If I have a drink, or two, or three… I'm not going to get into trouble. It's no problem for me because no one else can tell me what to do.

Another great thing about living on your own is that you can have a relationship. If I meet someone, I like to get to know the person. At some point, I might invite them back home. If we decide to have sex – or not – is nobody else's business. No one can tell me how to live my life, and no one can tell me if I can get married or not.

My life is totally different to Suzan's. Suzan is a friend of mine with a learning disability who uses a wheelchair. That's why she lives in a care home. Suzan has no freedom where she lives because she always needs to ask the care home staff if she wants to go out or have some friends around. Because staff think everything's a risk, she can't do the things I do. She can't choose who wakes her up or what time to wake up; she can't choose what she wants for her breakfast or dinner; she can't go out to see her friends or have her friends come round.

Suzan's world is very small and controlled. It'll never get any bigger. If Suzan has a relationship with anyone, she can't take them back home because there's a big issue around intimate relationships. Suzan can't choose to go to the cinema, or to the pub, or to meet up with her friends. The care home staff won't let her have a job because of the health and safety issues. Suzan will never have the chance to work abroad. She has no power to decide. But everybody else has the power to make decisions for her. What is most unfair is that I know what Suzan's life is like (because I had a time in my life when I had no power to make decisions), but Suzan will never know what it's like to have my life.

You wouldn't know it now, but a long time ago I was like a doormat. Although I've been working most of my adult life, I wasn't always as confident as I am now. I always knew I wanted to work, because having my own wage made me feel independent and happier. I didn't want to volunteer or rely on others. I wanted to do my own thing and be my own man. I didn't have any qualifications when I left school (they don't teach you much at special school), but I got a job as a trainee hotel porter and then moved onto housekeeping work and handyman jobs at the hotel. I enjoyed it because I was meeting new people and earning my own wage. I felt like a proper adult.

A charity that helps people with learning disabilities look for work got me my next job. The thing is, they get you a job and they think that this will make you happy, but you can feel forgotten. They got me work in a warehouse and the first year was fine. My job was sweeping up, packing and taking boxes to the skip. The warehouse boss didn't trust me to do anything else. I started to get very bored. Most of the time I was getting the job nobody wanted to do. I asked to do stock control; I was slow at it but I found it interesting and I hoped I could do more. I told the manager that I quite liked numbers and maths; I liked the order in numbers. But I was too slow; they said they didn't have time to support me to do that and they never let me do it again. The manager felt he'd ticked the box though, because he'd said yes. I wanted to challenge myself, but if you have a learning disability, employers think you can't do anything. The bosses don't want to train you, so you end up with a boring, tedious job.

The other blokes in the warehouse used to abuse me physically and mentally because of my disability. They used to call me – and I hate these words – 'retard' and 'spacca' (as in 'spastic'). They'd mock me because I used to stutter quite badly. They'd imitate me talking because of my speech impediment. I hated that job because for the next five years I was bullied, ridiculed and abused. The first time someone said something to me I was on the second floor of the warehouse, pulling boxes off shelves. I heard 'retard' from behind me, someone calling out. I said, 'What?' like I couldn't believe what I was hearing. Another time, someone lobbed a shoe at me and it got me in the head. I wanted to punch them, but I didn't want to lose my job. They used to throw boxes at me too. I asked them why and they said, 'We were joking.' I told them I didn't find it funny.

I thought, *I'm going to be here all my life and I'm never going anywhere*. I told the charity that had helped me get the job, but because I only saw the support worker there twice a year, nothing got done about it. I'd tell the manager and it'd get better for a week or two, but then it would get worse again. Every time I reported the abuse, I thought, *What's the point?* I'd get called 'grass'. I just felt like the other workers didn't want me there because of my learning disability. I was just someone to be abused.

I used to get very down and I felt very small, like I was less of a human being. I thought, *I'll be nothing*. I felt like I had nothing to aim for. I couldn't afford to leave because I needed the money. I was a dad by then and I needed that £100 a week, so I had to stick it out because of my kids and partner at the time, and I wanted to be independent. I'm a proud man; I didn't want to be on the dole. I had to prove my dad wrong, because he thought I was a loser. I wanted to prove to the world I could do a job and live on my own. I used to cry when I got home, but I'd think at least it was another day done. I'd tell my partner about it – I'd break down and say, 'I can't take another day.' The kids didn't know anything about it – they were too young.

It was a really dark time. I was dying inside.

Eventually I heard about a job going at CHANGE through the support charity that had got me the warehouse job. I got an interview. The interview was quite laid-back, which put my mind at rest. There were two people with learning disabilities on the panel, which made me feel equal and respected. They asked me about my experiences. I told them I had no A-levels, but I had experience of life as a father with a learning disability and I was passionate about our rights.

When I heard I'd got the job, I went into the warehouse with the biggest grin on my face. The last few days they tormented me because I was leaving. They tied me up with sticky tape and put a sock in my mouth. They said, 'It's just fun.' I told them, 'I don't find it funny, I'm not laughing.' After twenty or thirty minutes they untied me and told me I should be able to take a joke. They kept saying, 'You'll be back here,' because they thought I'd fail at the next job, and I thought, *No, I bloody won't*. I felt I was escaping from the hole I was in.

I like to think of my MBE as two fingers to the blokes at that warehouse.

When I got the job at CHANGE I felt like I'd won the lottery. I felt happy and equal. Before I got the new job, I didn't know what ambition was. I eventually lost my stutter because I developed confidence through working. In the past I didn't use the telephone because I thought people wouldn't understand me, but I do now.

Before this job I'd never been further than South Yorkshire – I'd never been to Leeds before. Now I travel all over the world to support young people and this builds my confidence. (I've become so confident through working, I've even travelled to the Philippines on holiday on my own.) I feel I'm more outspoken and confident because of what I do for a living. My reading and writing's better too. I've also co-authored a book called *Leaving Institutions, Voices for Change*, that aims to help social workers involved in moving people out of long-term residential care.

I think that without work I'd be very timid, isolated and lonely, and I wouldn't have a voice. The best thing about my job is that it's helped me challenge people in a way that's professional.

I can't read or write very well, but you can get around that. Apps on computers mean I can dictate my emails. The apps may not always understand my Yorkshire accent, but I can't help that. I get government funding to help disabled people in work; it's called Access to Work and it pays for someone to help with paperwork two mornings a week.

Before working at CHANGE, I was the only person with

a learning disability in my workplace. But at CHANGE, we have three staff with learning disabilities and eight staff without learning disabilities. We all develop our skills and interests instead of just being put into menial jobs. Working here means looking at the things you can do rather than what you can't do. People with and without disabilities work together in partnership. This is what's called 'inclusive employment' and it means people with learning disabilities are hired in senior, paid roles and we work alongside our co-workers who don't have disabilities. Everyone's equal.

The work we do at CHANGE is important because people can see people with learning disabilities working and running training workshops. This proves we can have a paid job and it's good because people aren't used to seeing people like us in power.

It's good for an organisation to have a team made up of people with and without learning disabilities. A person with a learning disability has a lot of life experience and skills that he or she can share with the person without a disability. I have to think about my colleagues without a disability, and they have to see me as an equal member of the team – not as what they call a 'service user', which is the term used in social care for people who need support. We get to really understand each other's experiences. We might not have A-levels, but we have life experience that makes us good at working together, and my knowledge of living with a learning disability is something you can't learn.

One of my best memories is when I went to a conference in Croatia about moving people out of institutions. I went with Catherine, a colleague with a learning disability, and it was just the two of us. Other people with learning disabilities aren't used to seeing people like us on our own. They're used to seeing us with support workers. A few people asked, 'Where's your support worker?' and I said, 'We haven't got one – we're proper paid workers.'

At first they didn't believe us; I saw their faces drop and they were gobsmacked. It was quite amusing. Then they started to question why they didn't have proper paid jobs themselves. I felt proud and equal, like I was challenging what usually happens. It's important for other people with learning disabilities to see what we can do, especially the younger people. People with learning disabilities are getting fed up of always doing volunteering or I talk to people I know who work really hard and only get twenty quid.

At the conference I was talking to a woman from Croatia, and when I told her about my children and family, she was crying because I gave her hope. I visited the Czech Republic, Bulgaria and Moldova to train health and social care professionals on how to support people to move into their own homes and to mentor young people in care to speak up for what they want.

A young lady from Bulgaria said, 'I want to be like you.' She used to live in an institution and wanted to be a role model. And since I first met her, that's exactly what she's done, because she mentors children moving out of care. All I did was pass the torch on to her. It's like a snowball effect: I support her, and she supports other people. It's been amazing to see her confidence grow, and she said it was because of me. She told me, 'It was you, Shaun; it was seeing how you work.' She's going to go far.

I went to Moldova to train some young people in public speaking. Two of the young people were quite shy, but they asked me loads of questions. A few months later, they were preparing to visit London and asked if I'd support them during their visit. But in the end, they didn't need my support much at all, they were so confident. When I first meet people like these young people, they tend to be very quiet and timid. Then as I spend time with them I see them becoming more aware of everything around them. Seeing someone I've mentored and been a role model to makes me happy and so proud. It's about supporting people to find their voice and the confidence to express themselves.

Being a role model for other people is one of the things I'm proudest of, because it's about getting young people to believe in themselves. I think I'm a good role model because I support people and I'm honest and passionate. I love having a job where people respect me and I like being part of something bigger than myself. Being a role model is like being a father and seeing your children grow.

Of course, being a father and grandfather is an achievement. I've got two grown-up children in their twenties – a son and daughter – and a fifteen-year-old daughter, who lives with my former partner in Sheffield. My daughter says, 'My dad works to make things better for people with learning disabilities.' I like to help people, and

I find that people open up to me. I listen to people a lot and they trust me. I like listening to my friends who have problems and at work my nickname's Father Shaun.

Parenting is hard work and I had to grow up really quickly. But seeing your kids walking, crawling, looking at you, you can't beat that. At my special school the only sex education we had was a cartoon; they didn't talk about sex or masturbation, or gay, lesbian, bisexual and transgender issues. Luckily for me, my mum talked to me about sex. She was open-minded. When I became a dad, I was working at the warehouse and the first thing I got asked was, 'Has the baby got a learning disability?' They asked this even before they asked if we'd had a boy or a girl. None of my kids have disabilities, but if they did, it wouldn't be a big deal. It's just a label people put on you.

What gets me annoyed is that people are surprised I have sex. It's like they're thinking, *What are you doing having sex?* We do have sex, yeah. If you have a learning disability people think you don't have sex, you don't understand the word love, that you look ugly. I do know what love is; I do know what sex is. I have a girlfriend.

People think if we have sex we're being cruel by having kids because they'll automatically have a learning disability and then their kids will have a learning disability. That's not the case and even if it was, big deal. Kids with a learning disability are human beings; they have a right to a life, to have a job, to live independently, to have relationships. If people don't like the fact we have kids, they can stick it. It's like eugenics – they don't want you to have kids.

I know people with learning disabilities who've gone to massage parlours because they don't know how to have relationships. They're lonely because their special schools didn't talk about things like sex education, so they don't feel confident about relationships and sex.

If I think about success, one of the first-ever wins for me was going on a bus to get to a cinema in Sheffield I'd never been to before. That was my first big try at being independent, without people doing it for me. It wasn't very long after I moved into my own place and I planned it all with my support worker. I went to the bus garage in Rotherham on my own and asked how often the buses went and from which platform. I had to work out the different bus stops, how long it would take to get there. The trip took forty-five minutes. I got one bus from my flat to the station, another one to the cinema, and then another two buses back. I felt like a kid at a birthday party after I'd done that; I felt really proud. Funny thing was that it was to see *Street Fighter*, that Jean-Claude Van Damme martial-arts movie. God, it was a pants film, although that wasn't the point of the day.

Going to the cinema was a big adventure for me, but since then I've been everywhere for work from Eastern Europe to Thailand and Sweden, Switzerland, Nicaragua and Ramallah in Palestine. In all these countries I was training professionals to work better with children and young people with learning disabilities, and supporting the young people to speak up for themselves. I've also been to Florida on holiday twice. I couldn't have done that before the job I have now, as I didn't have the confidence or the money.

I wish the older Shaun could go back to the younger Shaun and tell him what I've done. I'm not sure the younger Shaun would believe him.

Something that's difficult when you travel is that when you ask for help, people get the wrong idea about what you can and can't do. When I went to Croatia through Manchester, the airport staff were trying to be helpful, but they offered me a wheelchair when all I wanted was to be guided to the right bit of the airport. You have to laugh, though I was pretty pissed off at the time. It was the same in Croatia. My colleague Catherine and I had called ahead and said we need help with accessibility and maybe a guide to take us through, but I couldn't believe that there was an ambulance to meet us. I said, 'What do we need that for? We're not poorly.' I was angry; I don't swear, but I did then. I can walk, for crying out loud – I have a job and I work in England and around the world.

A similar thing happened at Tel Aviv airport when I told the person at the information desk that we needed guidance, and we were told we'd have to go in a wheelchair. I can laugh now, but it's wrong.

But I love the travelling. I've made new friends who I'd never have met otherwise. I've learned about other cultures and I feel like my world is expanding with every journey. So are my skills, friendships and knowledge. I want to do more public speaking about my personal story. I want to better other people's lives by going out there and telling people about my experience. I can't stop buzzing about it. That's what I love, doing different things like workshops, speaking and campaigning.

The one thing that can improve life for people with learning disabilities is attitudes. Some people and the media think that we're lazy or spongers, but we're not, we're hard-working people and we want the opportunity to have a job like everyone else. The trouble with people's attitudes is because they can't see our disability, they talk to us like babies or undermine us.

Some people get learning disability and mental health confused, and that needs to change. I talked to some Tory politicians at a conference once and it happened there. The politician said to us, 'Oh, you've got mental health problems,' and we said, 'No. We have learning disabilities. You're putting us all in one box and we're not happy about that.' I don't think they understand the difference between having a learning disability and having mental health issues.

I think that MPs need to be trained by us so that they can understand the difference and what support we might need. I'm really passionate about politics and all I could think of was that they're running the country and they don't know the difference. They should be working with us even before they become MPs, and that way they might learn to communicate better with ordinary people and particularly those of us with learning disabilities.

In companies or organisations like the NHS they should use those people who are already working there with a learning disability to give advice on accessibility. In a hospital, for example, there might be a porter with a learning disability who could help. If there are no workers with a learning disability in the organisation, then that needs to change as well. Here's an example. I went with my mum to the hospital. It took us twenty minutes to find where we had to go. There was no accessible signage with pictures so that we could understand where to go, no staff to help us. There was no colour coding like they have on the London Underground to help us get to where we had to go.

Here's another example. I was diagnosed with type 2 diabetes. I wanted to do the right thing with my diet, but I found it difficult. I couldn't understand any of the information I was given at my doctor's surgery. My colleague Catherine was the one who helped me. She has diabetes as well and she was able to support me by telling me how to spot the signs of problems with my blood sugar and explaining to me about diet in a way that I could understand. This is the kind of peer-to-peer support that we need to do more often.

What we need is a choice of what home we get. We need to be included in deciding what kind of home we want, where we want to live. If you need support workers, you need the opportunity to choose your support worker, and they need to listen to you and make sure you're included in everything. We need to make sure that people are living independently and have control over their lives. People still think that people with learning disabilities can't do anything, so we need to educate people.

One way to do that is by having more integration of children with learning disabilities into mainstream education.

I'm passionate about inclusive education and would like to push for more of it. And I think people with learning disabilities should maybe go to schools and talk about themselves to show we're just people like everybody else.

We need to promote more people with jobs who inspire other people. We need to be in the media and on TV – and not just in news stories about benefits and tragedies, like care scandals. We're an easy target and it's not right. We need to fight back. Now I'm starting to see the change, people like us becoming more powerful. I'm seeing people with learning disabilities being more outspoken and not standing for it any more. In some grassroots organisations like charities, I see people with learning disabilities having a bigger say. We're sick and tired of being put down all the time; people like us want to be respected, to have proper paid jobs and show that we've got families. We don't want to be isolated and to be living on benefits all the time; we want to live in a proper community and be parents. We work, we're independent, we work abroad, we have sex, we've got families and we've got mates.

All forms of media need to look at how people are doing things, breaking down barriers, and that will stop hate crime against people with learning disabilities. That is why we need to show what people are good at. We want people to stop feeling sorry for us. I want organisations to take people with learning disabilities more seriously for the skills they have, not just tokenistic things. CHANGE helped show me skills I didn't know I had. Lots of people with learning disabilities have hidden skills. I want other people to have that chance too. We're hard-working people and we want the opportunity to have a job like everybody else. We've got jobs, we're living on our own, we're part of the community. We're human beings just like you – we're not different.

My message is this: I'm a person with a learning disability who came from nowhere, with no power and no self-respect. I didn't know about my human rights. Other people with learning disabilities can achieve great things too. Never stop believing in yourself; don't let other people tell you that you can't do it. If you've got something you want to do, then do it. I think before you try and inspire others to believe in themselves, you have to believe in yourself first.

And don't take any crap.

———————————

Shaun Webster is a father, grandfather and human rights campaigner who was awarded an MBE in 2015 for services to people with learning disabilities and their families. As an international project worker with the human rights charity CHANGE, he works all over the UK and overseas as a speaker and trainer. He advises employers and governments, and health, social care and charity professionals on issues such as improving employment for learning-disabled people and promoting sex and health education. He is the co-author of the book *Leaving Institutions, Voices for Change*, which aims to help social workers involved in moving people out of institutions, and he is also a trustee of the housing support charity KeyRing.

@ChangeShaun

Champagne, Snakes and Stealing Chips

Sarah Gordy, MBE

I'm a woman and an actor first. I have Down's syndrome, but that's not all I am. There is so much more to me than my disability.

I'm a professional actor – I'm not 'professionally Down's syndrome'. The highlights of my acting career have been roles that aren't just about disability. The play *Jellyfish* by Ben Weatherill premiered in June 2018 at the Bush Theatre in London. It was more about love and relationships than disability. I helped Ben develop the story and the character of Kelly. Although my life experience has been very different, Ben used some of my character traits and my emotional acting range. Kelly's a woman who refuses to be told what to do and who to love. She wants to love who she wants and live her life. I love how she is.

In 2014 I was cast as a character without a learning disability. The play, *Crocodiles*, at the Royal Exchange

Theatre in Manchester, had nothing to do with disability, and neither did my character, Matilda. I played a wife and mother in a seaside town in the north of England.

In many of the other projects I've worked on, the roles have been focused on the challenges of having a learning disability. I've played characters in period TV dramas, like Lady Pamela Holland in *Upstairs Downstairs* in 2010 or Sally Harper in *Call the Midwife* in 2014, both on the BBC. These roles are important too, because they show how people like me used to be treated in an appalling way.

In the 1930s people were ashamed to have a relative with Down's syndrome. My character in *Upstairs Downstairs* was the sister of the lead character, Sir Hallam. It made me really sad that Lady Pamela was shut away for years in a private hospital and her brother was told she had died. The woman I played in *Call the Midwife* was in love with a young man who lived in the same institution as her in the 1950s. They were having a baby, but they weren't allowed to be together.

Thankfully, people's attitudes have got better since those days, but it's still not perfect. At the start of my career, I could tell that crews were worried that I couldn't do the role. When I turned up on set, I could see that the directors weren't sure if I'd understand what they wanted me to do, even though I'm as flexible as any other actor. Then there were stage managers and assistant directors wondering how they'd keep to a tight production schedule with an actor who had a learning disability. But by the end of each project, they wanted to work with me again.

I remember one job, where we were filming in real time with a narrator and several cameras, plus a live audience. I could tell that the assistant director was worried the minute he saw me. I knew he thought I was going to make loads of mistakes or be unreliable. But afterwards he said how thrilled he was with my performance, and that he felt bad that he'd thought I couldn't perform the role properly. It made me feel great to have proved him wrong and to know that we respected each other.

This is a job – if I wasn't good then I wouldn't get any work. I'm successful because I prepare for my roles, I know my lines, I turn up on time and I stick to the schedule. I completely commit to every project and I earn respect. If I'm offered a part, I spend a couple of days talking it over with my mum, Jane, who's also my personal assistant and acting coach. It's so important to me to be professional; other people's jobs are depending on me and I don't want the show or filming to fall behind schedule because of something I've done. Everyone on a production is relying on me to do the best possible job, so once I commit to a show, I'm not going to do anything other than work hard and be fantastic. No director's ever going to expect less of me just to be nice. So you've got to be good at what you do.

One of the best compliments I've had came from another actor who I was in a play with. She said, 'Sarah is a safe pair of hands.' She meant that when we're all out on stage, everyone can trust me. So if someone has a wobble, the other actor will help them along. I did this when an actor got first-night nerves and forgot her words – I just had to help her with a little prompt so she remembered the next line.

I don't think you can teach someone to be a great actor. Being able to act is something you have or you don't. I think the reason I've been successful is because I was born with a talent for acting, and I also work hard. If you want to act, you shouldn't think of it only as a career – you should be doing it for the joy of it. It's a good way of learning about life. You learn to walk in someone else's shoes when you play a role. If you really can do that, then there's a chance you can be a good actor.

I think success is also about making work a positive experience. And success *is* the performance. That's what actors live for. The performance is the only thing that matters, at the end of the day. You need to be completely determined to deliver that performance and make it real. Every character I play feels real to me. I live the role while I'm on stage or filming, I don't pretend. I feel the emotions of the character and if I really believe that what I'm feeling is real, then the audience can too. I make sure I know the character's history and personality, so I can understand everything about them. That way the character is real to me and I can 'be' her, not just play her. I actually feel lonely without a character and a story in my head.

Some actors I've worked with say that what I do is 'method acting', but I'm not sure I'd call it that. All I know is that I have to feel and 'be' the person I'm playing to do my job well, and to get the audience to believe in the character. It's a bit like method acting, but not as extreme because I come out of the character as soon as I've done a scene. I've worked with actors who stay in character all the time and I couldn't do that.

My mum says my approach is like there are two computer programs running at the same time in my head. One is mine; one is my character's. I can drop one and take up the other when a scene starts or ends. I do breathing exercises and say my character's name, or my name, to switch between one 'program' and the other. I don't like auditions because it feels like pretending for a few minutes, instead of actually being the character and living her life.

The way Mum describes it, I don't 'act' but I live another life. I do think that feeling a character is the key to my success. Once, I was talking to an actor about Shakespeare's plays and he told me, 'You really *feel* Shakespeare.' A lot of people want to show off how much they know about Shakespeare, but no one really wants a lesson. They want to enjoy the plot and the people he wrote about. Shakespeare didn't write for people to study his words in detail. He wrote to make people laugh and cry and feel.

I fell in love with Shakespeare when I saw *Henry IV Parts I and II* in 2005 at the National Theatre in London. It starred Michael Gambon and David Bradley, and it was just incredible. I absolutely fell in love with the language and the story. *Romeo and Juliet* is my favourite play. I got to know it well when I played a character called Mary, a maid, in a touring show called *Seize the Day* a few years ago. My character had to quote from *Romeo and Juliet*. I love the scene when Juliet's waiting for Romeo in the orchard after they've secretly got married. She's waiting for night-time so they can be together and she's thinking of how handsome he is. Juliet's words are just beautiful and she's so completely in love with Romeo. I love that speech and I can recite it by heart. This is the part I love best, from Act III, Scene II:

Come, gentle night; come, loving black-browed night,
Give me my Romeo; and when I shall die,
Take him and cut him out in little stars,
And he will make the face of heaven so fine
That all the world will be in love with night.

Sometimes, I dream in my character and about the world of the character I'm playing. That's because when I'm in a production, I spend each night going over and over the next day's scenes. It's the last thing I think of at night and what's in my head when I wake up. Mum says I talk in my sleep. Sometimes she hears me rehearsing lines for the next morning or else she'll hear me mention the names of the other characters.

Every character I play also has a smell; I decide what scent would suit them, and that helps me prepare for the role. I wear the scent and it helps me become them. When I played Matilda in *Crocodiles*, I decided that her scent was mint and jasmine because her character is sensitive and innocent but lives in a harsh place. Jasmine and mint smell lovely, and can both grow in difficult conditions, so it made sense for her to have a combination of both those scents. Kelly in *Jellyfish* smelled of apricots from her shampoo.

For the role of Sally Harper in *Call the Midwife*, I asked my mum to email the show's writer, Heidi Thomas, to get some more background on the character. This was the East End of London in the 1950s, so does she smell of perfume, and is she posh? Or does she smell of carbolic soap, which was used for washing and cleaning at the time, so she's a respectable working-class girl? Or maybe she smells of dirt and cabbage? Heidi told us my character would have got perfume for a gift, and worn it on special occasions like Christmas, but usually she'd smell of carbolic soap. Just that tiny bit of information helped me bring the character to life.

In *Upstairs Downstairs*, I gave my character, Lady Pamela, a perfume, Blue Grass by Elizabeth Arden, that was first introduced in 1934. It's a flowery smell that a young lady would wear.

I research my characters really well too. For *Upstairs Downstairs*, I read history books to find out how people like me were treated in the 1930s. They'd lock up people with disabilities like prisoners. I went to my local library to look at old newspapers to see what life would have been like back then. I decided that Lady Pamela was lonely and isolated but she was also a strong and loyal woman; she had to be after being hidden away from her family for so long. She missed her brother so much and it was her love for him that kept her going.

When I'm getting ready for a role, Mum helps me rehearse with trigger words to bring out certain emotions. I love champagne. It's my favourite drink. So say 'champagne' and I feel the fun and joy of a party and smile brightly – we call it my 'champagne smile'. I don't like snakes, so if you say 'snakes', I'm horrified. I think it's very unfair to steal anybody's chips. If I've got a plate of chips, I don't want anyone taking them! Say 'stealing chips' and I'll feel shock and disgust.

The other thing that helps me do my work well is that I need to get hold of the script as early as possible to help me prepare. It's a reasonable adjustment to the process and costs nothing; it just takes a bit of planning and trust. Mum helps me learn my lines and understand the character relationships and history. Preparation is everything.

My mum's role in my success is key. She's not a trained acting coach but says she grew into what was needed. She knows how I work and what I need to do to bring a character to life. We have been talking about me possibly working with other creatives to support my acting work when Mum is busy. I live at home with my parents in Lewes, East Sussex, so Mum's always on hand to help me develop and rehearse a role, but she can't do my job for me; she can't act it. She helps me with my lines, with what the director might say or ask. She's laid the foundations that mean I can go on and do what I want to do and am good at. She is passionate about the quality of my performance and I get my determination from both her and my dad, Jere. They're both so supportive and proud of my work.

I grew up surrounded by words, with lots of books, reading together and telling stories. My mum says that when

I was growing up, I found it easier to understand ideas if they were explained to me as stories. She's always said that storytelling is a great way of telling people about life, like the stories in Aesop's Fables. Home was a place that allowed me to develop my talent. It started when my younger sister, Catherine, and I were toddlers. We'd sit at the kitchen table in our old house in Bromley, Kent, listening to stories Mum and my grandma, Maggie, would tell. Sometimes my sister and I would tell each other stories. Mum would watch over us, encourage us or join in with our stories as she cooked or washed up.

Catherine and I are really close – we're only sixteen months apart – so we'd make up characters and give them personalities and backstories and put on little shows. We'd make masks and hats and involve Mum and Dad or the rest of the family if they were around. It was fairy stories in the early days; Catherine and I would be princesses. I was Princess Moonbeam, Catherine was Princess Sunbeam (because of the colour of her hair – she was blonder than me as a child). Mum was Duchess. Grandma was High Queen, our uncles were dukes protecting us from dragons and other fantastic beasts. We'd always return to the same characters as well as make up new ones, and each time we'd add a bit more to the character. Now we are grown up, Catherine manages my website and helps all the family with her technical expertise. I can talk about anything with her. I am so lucky to have her.

My sister says she always tears up when I perform. Whether the role I play is funny or sad, she's so proud of me that at the end of every show, even ones that she has seen before, she's always crying as well as clapping. When we were little we would play and fight as other siblings do, but my sister was always there to help me. I learned a lot from her. And she says she learned a lot from me too. She got to meet lots of different people growing up. She saw that sometimes people didn't know how to act around me and my friends. She is always looking out for me and says how sad it is that people miss out on so much because they close themselves off from new and different things. They also miss out by underestimating what I can do. I've spoken about this in some of the talks I've done as part of my campaigning work for Mencap. We shouldn't underestimate what people are capable of. We should lose the labels.

At primary school I was at my happiest acting in the plays and I also liked helping the other kids when they were on stage. There was one nativity play when I was playing Mary, but one of my classmates was a sheep and got stage fright. I went up to her and said, 'You're such a lovely sheep,' stroked her, and she came back up on stage. The stage just felt normal to me, not a scary place, and I thought everyone should be able to enjoy performing.

After primary school, we moved to America for four years because of Dad's work. I went to middle school in Texas then we came back to the UK. I went to mainstream schools, not special schools. Like many people I had mixed experiences at school. I had some good teachers (especially at primary school) and some not so good. I liked going to school and being with the other children. I acted in school plays, but that was because it was fun, not because I thought acting was what I'd do when I grew up.

Back in England, I did a drama course at a local college, but it wasn't very challenging, so I started looking for other chances to act. A theatre group for people with learning disabilities auditioned me and said I was great but that another girl fitted their type of work better. Later, however, when ITV were searching for an actor to do a complicated role, the theatre group put my name forward.

This was my first break, a role in an episode of the ITV series *Peak Practice*, playing a teenager with Down's syndrome. I rehearsed everything from the facial expressions I'd use to each movement I'd make, and even where I'd pause for breath. I loved being on set, being with the other actors, and it was an incredible feeling to know that the cast and crew felt I'd done a great job. I knew this was what I wanted to do. I knew I'd never be an accountant – I have no idea about numbers – and here was something I could do, and do well. After that, I told Mum I wanted to take my acting seriously – I wanted to be a professional actor. It wasn't about being famous. Right from the start I just wanted to act – and to act really well. I carried on with the local drama groups and got an agent, and after that the television and theatre work began coming in.

When I heard from my agent that I'd got the role in *Upstairs Downstairs*, I was volunteering at my local charity shop, the British Heart Foundation. I like being a volunteer because I like helping people, and I love being involved in the local community. I burst into tears when my agent told me the news; I was over the moon because it was my dream to do a costume drama. I love vintage dresses and I love history.

Sometimes being on set can be a long, intense day, so it's important to know how to relax. I watch television, usually drama or films. I don't like most reality television, but I like *Strictly Come Dancing* because I love dance. I also love looking stuff up on the internet or playing games on my iPad. I like to read too. Sometimes about history, sometimes Shakespeare. I read books connected to the roles I play. I love Jennifer Worth's memoir, *Call the Midwife*, on which the show is based.

I love singing too, although I sound very flat. I absolutely love karaoke on a night out. I also get to go to a lot of parties through work – I love a good party and I love dancing. At parties, I like to have a drink too – champagne, of course!

I perform with the dance company Culture Device Project. I don't get paid for this, but I do it in my spare time. I like to improvise in my dance, and it helps me express myself. I'm very polite and gentle, but when I do dance improvisation I can be more bold, and express feelings like violence or passion through my body. That makes me feel very free.

I've worked hard to get where I am today, and I'm proud of my success. However I would like to see more diversity on stage and screen. As part of my role as a celebrity ambassador for the learning disability charity Mencap I'm campaigning to change this. I'm proud to be the charity's first celebrity ambassador with a learning disability. I've had meetings with MPs about how to get more people with learning disabilities to vote, and I've opened the Belfast City Marathon.

In 2015 I was invited to speak at Mencap's second annual Lord Rix Lecture. The lectures are named in memory of the late actor, activist and Mencap campaigner Lord Brian Rix and always deal with subjects that are important to people with learning disabilities and their families. I talked about the need for more people with learning disabilities to be cast and for more positive representation of people with learning disabilities on screen.

In 2017, I supported Mencap's campaign to highlight the lack of representation of actors with disabilities at the Oscars. At the time, the 'Oscars So White' campaign was showing how there wasn't much racial diversity in film, but no one was talking about how people like me are represented. Did you know that 16 per cent of Oscars are awarded to non-disabled actors playing a disabled character? Or that only 12 per cent of the public say they have seen someone with a learning disability in a film?[1] I think that to be good, drama has to reflect the world as it is. Does everyone look the same? Does everyone sound the same? Does everyone move the same? Is everyone 'perfect'? No. People with learning disabilities are part of our society – there are 1.5 million of us in the UK – so it's important that we're seen on television, in theatre and film, and heard on radio.

Often, if you do see an actor with a learning disability, they're in a role to do with the problems their disability creates. Although this can be a good way of raising awareness, or showing how we mustn't go back to the bad way people used to be treated, the character appears as a 'disability', not as a 'woman'. You never see 'non-issue' roles played by an actor who has a learning disability, like someone working in a newsagent, or on a reception desk. It would be great to see actors like me portraying someone who's ordinary, just part of society and real life. I have had some wonderful characters before, but they are often very dependent. Why can't we see someone doing something other than just 'being' learning disabled? I'd like to see more small parts played by people with learning disabilities. It would be great if more film and theatre people had the attitudes of the team I worked with for *Crocodiles*, the play where my character didn't have a disability. We want the acting world to look at the person, not the disability.

One of the best characters I've played is Kelly in *Jellyfish*. She is a woman first, before her disability, and she's a strong, funny and passionate human being, living a full life. The writer, Ben, told me that he'd been watching me since I was on *Holby City* years ago, when I played a patient with a learning disability. He's a big fan of mine. Ben said that since then, he'd wanted to write about a character who was different and a character who didn't just represent a learning disability.

People with learning disabilities notice if the only role that learning-disabled actors ever play are defined by their 'special need'. A while ago, I was in my local supermarket when a young guy who has a learning disability came up to me. Adam worked at the supermarket and said he'd seen me on *Holby City*. He said, 'Sarah, you were brilliant on television yesterday, but you're not doing us any favours. Your characters are always helpless and sad. Please play a character with a job, a life and giggles.' Adam wanted to see someone on screen who was like him – someone who's happy, an ordinary person, with a job, a life and friends.

What Adam said made me feel a bit embarrassed, but what could I say? I feel like I'm changing perceptions by being out there, but of course I agree it'd be better if I could play other kinds of roles. I'm trying my best. I felt like I'd let him down, but I don't commission the shows or cast the roles – I don't rule the world. I also need to take on acting jobs, so if I turned down those roles, I'd have no work.

Luckily there are writers like Ben who wrote *Jellyfish* who are willing to go the extra mile and change how learning disability is seen on stage. We need the people who commission the television and theatre productions to do more. I want to challenge them to knock down the stereotypes that appear on television and in films. The writers and producers have the ideas, so it's the bosses who need to have faith in doing something differently. And if we got more people behind the scenes too – working in production, doing camerawork – that would help.

I think more people with learning disabilities should get involved with the media too, so the public can see us more and read about our lives. A lot of people only think negative things when they hear or read the words 'learning disability'. There are too many negative headlines, and the positive stuff about people's talents gets left out. I think things are improving, but it's too slow.

Journalists write about what I do, or I get interviewed about my work on television, and that's positive. But there are a whole lot more people out there, like Adam, who are independent and have great lives. They have a job, their own place to live and a busy social life. A successful life isn't always about opening nights and champagne! It's not like my life as an actor is constantly glamorous; there's a lot of intensive rehearsing and, frankly, some of the digs I stay in are quite rough and ready.

In 2016 I modelled for the fashion photographer Rankin as part of a campaign he shot for Mencap, 'Here I Am'. I loved the message of the 'Here I Am' campaign: 'Learning disability has been invisible for too long. It's time to see people with a learning disability for all they are and all they can be.' Rankin created these beautiful images of lots of different people and it was amazing to be a part of it. It wasn't about being on billboards or posters or anything; I did it because I want people to think twice about people like me. Even if I'm doing a modelling job, I'm still playing a part and reacting to what the photographer wants me to do.

If newspapers, magazines and television news changed how they cover learning disability, it would do a lot to clear up confusion about it. Some people think it is a mental health issue, or it's an illness, or you can 'cure' it. I want people to know that learning disability is a lifelong condition and you need a bit of extra support, but it doesn't and shouldn't stop you from doing the things you'd like to do and are good at. There are different levels of learning disability, of course. I have Down's syndrome, but I am very capable of doing most things. Everyone is different and no two people with a learning disability are the same.

So there are barriers, but things have changed for the better since the days of Lady Pamela or Sally Harper. You can see how people with learning disabilities are treated much better. There are opportunities, but we need more of them, and there is still work to do on attitudes. My ambition is to play parts that have nothing to do with disability.

In the future, I want to be like my role model Dame Judi Dench. She's such an incredible actor and so great with people. I was lucky enough to meet her when I performed at a Down's Syndrome Association event. I was totally starstruck and inspired by how generous and respectful she is with other artists. She was so great as M in the Bond films, and she's been acting for sixty years, which inspires me. I hope that I have as long a career in acting and can encourage other people to do what they are good at and follow their dreams.

I have a great life. I love hanging out with interesting, creative people, people who trust me, who I trust and can work with to create something new and fresh for audiences. My dad, Jere, once said, 'The best ideas come from the left field.' He was talking about how more writers need to create interesting roles for disabled actors, and the best stories aren't always the standard stories. Difference is good, that's exactly it. What the left field – which describes something unusual or different – can bring doesn't get enough credit. The positive things about learning disability don't usually get talked about. People have so much to offer. But this gets ignored. People need to see that it's not about the disability; it's about the person behind the disability. I like to think that by doing my job, by being seen, I'm changing people's views. And while I'm acting and campaigning, I'm really enjoying what I do. My life, and the lives of other people like me, can be busy and joyous, full of determination to do a good job and to have fun.

Sarah Gordy is an actor best known for critically acclaimed roles in BBC dramas *Upstairs Downstairs*, *Call the Midwife* and *The Silkworm*. Her stage, screen and radio roles include appearances in ITV's *Peak Practice* and BBC's *Holby City* and *Doctors*. Sarah starred as a character without a disability in Lee Mattinson's play *Crocodiles* at Manchester's Royal Exchange Theatre in 2014. She played the leading role in Ben Weatherill's critically acclaimed play *Jellyfish* at the Bush Theatre in London in 2018 and at The National Theatre in 2019.

In 2018 she became the first woman with Down's syndrome to be awarded an MBE for services to the arts and people with disabilities. In the same year, she was awarded an honorary doctorate by Nottingham University for her work in the arts and in campaigning. Sarah became Mencap's first celebrity ambassador with a learning disability in 2013. She has also been a patron of Circus Starr since 2015. Her pro bono work includes modelling, dancing with the company Culture Device Project and volunteering at a British Heart Foundation charity shop near her home in Lewes, East Sussex.

@sarah_gordy

Black Cats and Chemistry Sets

Gary Bourlet

Everyone has the right to speak up. To be treated like a normal person and a citizen, and to have rights. The moment I started thinking, *What can I do – why are we being ignored?* came on a wet and grey March day in London more than thirty years ago.

A hundred of us had been bussed to a council-run day centre for people with learning disabilities in Brent, north-west London, for the day. These places were meant to give you training – we were called 'trainees' – but there was never actually much in the way of skills on offer. It was more about containing people with learning disabilities in an institution. It was raining hard as we pulled in early, fifteen minutes before the centre opened. The drivers were ordering us off their coaches, but there was nowhere dry to wait so we were fighting to get back on board. It was a standoff. Then I saw the staff inside the day centre, warm and dry, drinking their morning coffees. I imagined them laughing about what they got up to at the weekend while we were shut out, wet and cold. I was furious, and also worried that some of the weaker among us might get pneumonia. That's when I decided to do something about it. I ran to the side entrance with another trainee, walked in and opened the front doors for everyone else.

I'm a campaigner and a self-advocate. A self-advocate is someone who speaks up for themselves about issues that are important to them. You represent yourself, you know your rights and you're more in control instead of having other people make decisions for you. I'm sixty years young, a gentleman who's polite and respectful, which means I like being courteous to people and seeing their good side. I think that's important if you want to be successful. I like to look at people and think, *That person's doing well*, or, *That person might need a bit more help to get to the next level.* I've got a glass-half-full approach to life.

I'm a person who has mild learning disabilities and epilepsy. I live alone, but have family scattered around the south-east of England. I have many friends, mostly made through the work that I do. I like going to the cinema and theatre, and I enjoy country and coastal walks. I like public speaking and meeting and greeting people – I'm a good communicator. Being part of a campaigning movement is like being part of a big social club, a club with a purpose.

I'm proud of having set up the first learning disability organisation in the UK led by learning-disabled people themselves. Learning Disability England is the first-ever charity and membership organisation for people with learning disabilities as well as for their families, friends and people who work in care. We campaign for greater powers to be seen, to vote, to be included. We fight for human rights and for people to speak up for themselves. If the public sees more people with learning disabilities representing themselves in newspapers or on television, that'll change how society sees them. Our members include over 140 organisations from across England and 505 individual people with and without learning disabilities, everyone from relatives to carers to professors.

What we're doing is unique because people, families and organisations have always worked separately, but Learning Disability England connects up all the good work around the country and spreads it further. We're like a megaphone, taking people's voices and making them louder. 'Stronger, louder, together' is our slogan.

Around 300 people come to our annual conferences, which are led by people with learning disabilities and held in cities like Birmingham and Manchester. We want the same opportunities in our social life, education and employment as everyone else. Our campaigning priorities at Learning Disability England include opportunity and choice – not having the right support means people don't have control over their lives. Money's another concern. We give free advice to members on things like how to develop better housing and support for people, or information on benefits and the impact of welfare reform. Across the country, people are struggling on increasingly tighter budgets.

I've been doing this kind of work for decades, but I still never switch off. When my friends talk to me about their problems with their benefits, about how they struggle to get by because the government has cut their support, I get emotional. It's like I can feel their pain in my heart.

When I was a child growing up on a housing estate in north-west London, I had so many ideas about what I wanted to be when I grew up. I remember watching the moon landing on television, seeing Neil Armstrong become the first man on the moon. I wanted to be an astronaut. I had loads of toy cars and wanted to be a mechanic. My parents gave me a chemistry set and I was into science.

When you're a child you're always learning, always finding out what you want to be. It's natural for a child to want to be a bit adventurous. I was home-schooled until I was eight, because in the 1960s there was no proper school for 'mentally handicapped' children (that was the term used at the time). My tutor was a good, supportive woman. I still have the toy black cat she gave me as a gift. When I was younger, I thought that if I ever went to university, that'd be the mascot I'd take. That cat was a symbol of my future and what I might do. I look at it now and it takes me back to a happy time.

I've got good memories of the community where I lived: the front door being left open during the day so friends would come in and out, my parents swapping milk and sugar with the neighbours, my mum gossiping with next door. Ours was a close-knit family. My mum and dad, Bob and Josephine, would do big Sunday lunches; Dad would be carving the roast, and me and my four sisters made our own entertainment – these were the days before computers. The girls would skip; I'd play football outside with some of the other boys, even though ball games were banned on the estate, so we all disbanded when the caretaker caught us. I don't remember it all because the medication I was on to control my epilepsy made me sleepy during the day.

My dad worked for the Department of Health and Social Security, the government department that dealt with people's benefits. He helped people who'd applied for benefits, and he was quite visionary. He removed the glass panel on his desk that was meant to separate him from the people claiming benefits, because he didn't want that divide. I remember feeling proud, seeing him in his suit with his security badge and briefcase. I don't have memories of talking to Dad about the people he helped, but I suppose something of him – his vision – rubbed off onto me.

When I was eight, I started at the first school for autistic children run by Sybil Elgar in Ealing, west London. Mrs Elgar was an amazing woman; she was a pioneer of special schools, and helped found what went on to become the National Autistic Society. I'm not autistic, so I guess it was like fitting a square peg into a round hole, but there was nowhere else for me to go.

Back then, no one thought it was possible for children like me to go to a mainstream school. I enjoyed my time at the special school because the teachers were caring. Mrs Elgar was disciplined, very well spoken and kind, and she always got on well with us children. The teachers took us on picnics down to the coast and, because the school only had a dozen or so pupils, they had more time for each of us. We were individual little people, not just a big group to be managed or herded around. One of my school friends was deaf, and I wanted to learn sign language so I could communicate with him properly. I remember starring in a Christmas play – I was the wolf in *Peter and the Wolf*. I loved acting in front of the parents, learning the lines and rehearsing the show, and I didn't feel nervous. It was exciting. Things were rosy then. I was happy; I didn't want to leave.

School and qualifications are important if you want to be successful; they're part of building a career brick by brick. That's what I've done, although I got my qualifications after school. I did adult-education courses like management, word processing and personal effectiveness. That last one's important; it helps you recognise your abilities and make the most of them. Without confidence and proper training, someone with a learning disability goes into a job set up to fail. Everyone should be paid properly for their work too, not just be given endless work experience – it's free labour unless it has a purpose and it's paid.

'Not everyone wants to be a leader; you need the confidence, assertiveness and self-determination – this is about taking on responsibility and sometimes taking risks. Don't forget you're not just representing yourself, but you are representing lots of people's views.' I wrote those words for a report on leadership for a learning disability charity.

You don't become a leader overnight. First, you have to learn how to speak up for yourself. You have to know how to represent yourself before you start leading other people, and you need time to develop your skills. The key things are learning how to speak slowly and clearly. You also need presentation skills and you have to be able to speak to different-sized audiences and in different-sized venues. You need to build your self-esteem, self-worth and self-respect. You have to separate aggressiveness from assertiveness, because these two can get confused.

When I was thirteen, I had to leave Mrs Elgar's school. The local education authority sent me away to Derbyshire, 120 miles from home, to a residential school for children with behavioural problems. My parents had no say in where I went and were told there was no choice and nowhere closer. Caldwell Hall School was more like a borstal than a boarding school. I called it Colditz.

Children were meant to be seen but not heard, and we had to be good for over six weeks to gain our 'freedom' and be allowed home for the weekend. If you got into a fight, bunked off or answered back to teachers, you'd be constantly supervised by staff. But if you behaved well – kept quiet, did what you were told, followed orders – you'd get your freedoms, so you could play football, have a later bedtime or go out into the town centre.

Being there felt like a punishment. I didn't make any friends and there was nothing at that place to help you with any of your dreams. I wanted to learn chemistry, but we weren't allowed. I guess they were scared we'd do something wrong and blow up the school. It was all about what we couldn't do and I felt rubbished by the teachers. I especially hated Friday mornings because we had to do cross-country running. I was a skinny lad and, no matter if it was snowing or raining, all I was allowed to wear was a thin T-shirt and shorts. It was brutal.

Once, I had an epileptic fit at the local swimming baths and had to have my lungs pumped out in hospital. There was another incident when I was made to paint some fencing with creosote, a wood preservative that you can't buy today because it's so noxious. I was probably made to do it as some kind of punishment. Some of the chemical got into my eye and it was a few days before I could see properly again. No one thought to give me goggles for protection – there was no health and safety. I think it was the school wanting to save money and not really caring that it was dangerous.

This was the first time I'd been away from my parents. Days were like weeks and weeks were like months because I'd have to wait for so long to see them again. I missed my mum and dad so much. I wouldn't wish that experience on any child. I wish I'd had the confidence then to speak up and tell my parents how much I hated it. They didn't know, and I didn't tell Mum till I was thirty, by which time my dad had passed away. I didn't want them to feel bad and I thought that was the way it had to be. Mum would phone and send parcels filled with sweets and comics. I loved getting them, but it also made me feel even more that this was a prison and I was receiving packages from an outside world that I wasn't part of. I left that school at eighteen with no qualifications. I wasted my years there. If I'd had any ideas about what I wanted to do before going to that place, they were stamped out by the time I left.

After school I moved back home and started going to the day centre. My social worker told me I'd be there for six months. I was there for six years. I did gardening work and made paving slabs for £4 a week. Even then it was a rubbish wage. There was other so-called 'therapeutic work' too, which involved filling up plastic bags with screws, then packing those bags into boxes. We were just powerless, because staff had all the control. You were ordered to do a job without being told why. Even though we had a trainees' committee, it was a talking shop. We were told we could speak up, but it didn't count for anything.

A couple of us asked the managers if we could join the National Union of Students, but that horrified the parents' committee, which had a say in how the centre was run. Things are different now, but there was a time when parents didn't believe their son or daughter had a voice. Doctors told them, 'Your child won't achieve anything,' and they didn't challenge that. I asked for a drink-vending machine, so we could help ourselves when we felt thirsty, but my idea was turned down for being too expensive. Being rejected was a bitter pill to swallow. It felt like anything we suggested got automatically refused. You got no trust from the staff, you trusted no one and you couldn't complain. The place put me in a bad temper.

Walking into the centre one morning, I saw a poster for a new 'participation forum' run by the charity Mencap. The meeting was advertised as a chance for people who went to day centres in London to talk about what they thought of them. I was curious, so I went along. For the first time, it felt like we were able to speak up and our experiences were being shared and listened to. We all had a chance to speak freely without getting into trouble. I wasn't the only one angry about how we were treated and about not being able to speak my mind. We met every few weeks and we began to represent ourselves in our day centres without anybody else speaking for us. A guy called John Hersov, who worked at Mencap, helped us organise meetings and rehearse our speeches. He was about my age, very approachable and we got on really well.

The more involved I got in these meetings, the more confident I became. We'd discuss all the things that worried us, not just life at the day centres. Some people thought that staffing cuts on the London Underground would make it harder for people with disabilities to travel, because there'd be no one to ask for help. So we wrote to London Regional Transport, protesting against the job losses.

I suggested we try and run a training course for people to help them speak up for themselves. I knew some people at the day centres found reading hard, so we used pictures in our newsletters that meant they could understand the information. We debated the 'H' on people's bus passes, which showed they were handicapped. I used to wear this T-shirt with the slogan: LABEL JARS – NOT PEOPLE. I knew we needed to change the label if we were to change people's attitudes. I wanted to rub out the words 'mental handicap' and instead use the words 'a person with a learning disability'. Or better still, get people to call us by our names.

It wasn't like I worked on an idea one day and forgot about it the next. This stuff was with me all the time. Sometimes I couldn't even sleep because I was always thinking about the meetings and ideas. Even when I played pop music to relax, the ideas were all still going round in my brain.

I began leading the meetings, and John helped us organise bigger events to talk about our work and our ideas. Our seminars had titles like 'Speaking for Ourselves' and 'Have We a Future?' and were aimed at day-centre staff and people higher up like social services managers and civil servants, as well as people with learning disabilities. Around eighty people came to our first seminar and within two years we had a crowd of 280 at County Hall, which was then the headquarters of the Greater London Council. I was nervous when I spoke, but all I could do was be myself.

One of the first speeches I did was called 'Dull food makes dull minds'. For me, that was the beginning of my career. My dad helped me write my speech, but he passed away before he was able to hear it. I dedicated my speech to him. I watched the news to see how people speak on TV, to pick up ideas, and I was pleased to get applause when I finished. It was good to know people supported what I'd said.

We began getting invitations to do talks about our views and experiences from council social services departments. We'd talk mostly about day centres, but also about the use of labels or the benefits system. At one stage we were getting so many requests that we had to turn some of them down – that really was something, seeing as these were the sort of professionals who'd always had the power to say 'yes' or 'no'. Some of them would hear us speak and say things like, 'Ours couldn't do that,' meaning that our group was somehow unusual because we got our points across so well. They didn't think the learning-disabled people they knew could do that. But, as John said, no one thought, *This is what people can do if they're given time and encouragement*.

Looking back, the anger from my time at the residential school and the day centre was being channelled. It was going into proper action. That negative stuff shaped what I did. By now, in my slogan T-shirt, with my long, curly hair and beard, I'd become a bit of a rebel.

The old Gary had gone; Gary the campaigner was born.

'Dull food makes dull minds', 1985, by Gary Bourlet, dedicated to Bob Bourlet

In some centres the food has no flavour and no vitamins, which is bad for the trainees. It is boiled too long and it is mostly processed and frozen food. Food should look appetising and be cooked properly. Small portions are all right for smaller people, but some trainees are larger and have to eat what they get. Lunch is the main meal for lots of the trainees. They don't have enough money to go out and buy food. There should be a choice of foods (e.g. salads). Not too much sugar, and it must not be burnt. Junk food (like fried food) can affect the mind and cause behaviour problems. Trainees' behaviour patterns could change with the right diet, right vitamins and minerals, and nutrition. What can the council do about our food?

The first time I went on a plane, I went to America as part of a British delegation to a conference in Seattle. The conference was part of a new international movement called People First. It was called People First because the idea was that if you have a learning disability, you're a person first and someone with a disability second. I learned so much, and what I saw and heard over those five days changed my vision. We saw how the movement had taken hold in the States and in other countries like Canada and Sweden. Everyone shared a common cause. We had nothing like this back home – and I knew we had to be part of it. I made a speech about what speaking up about our rights meant to me. 'People should see us do something worthwhile,' I said. 'Campaigning,' I said, 'makes us feel like and be accepted as human beings, and not robots.'

I was impressed by how people from the other countries spoke and what they said. I heard stories about the abuse at places like Tranquille Sanatorium in British Columbia. Tranquille was used to house the 'mentally handicapped' until its closure, and the people who'd been locked up there were starting to talk publicly about the abuse they'd suffered. There were people crying because of the way they'd been treated in these big North American asylums. The authorities were trying to close them down and move people back to their own neighbourhoods to live in proper communities. I heard stories of people who'd died in these places, never having had the chance to get out.

Everyone who spoke talked with such confidence, like they were making political speeches. My head was spinning with ideas to take back home. I knew what it was that I wanted to do. Coming back on the jumbo jet, I said to my friends, 'We have to start a People First in our country.'

Back in London, with John's help, I organised the UK's first People First meetings in London. We had a bit of money from The King's Fund, a health and care charity. We only expected a small crowd, but word had spread and the tiny room was packed with thirty people. Some had to sit on the floor because we didn't have enough chairs. We had about fifteen items on the agenda, from how much of a say we had in how day centres were run to which conferences we might speak at and equal rights in education. In the end, it was so busy that we only got through a handful of the issues.

We started charging £1 a year membership and sent leaflets to hospitals, residential homes and special schools to publicise our work and try and attract more people. I wrote out 400 letters by hand, copying out random names and addresses from the phone book while Mum watched over me for support. I wanted to raise the profile of the organisation and get people to donate to our cause. I paid for the stamps from my benefit money. I was doing it because I had to. I can't remember if we got any money from those letters, but I do remember just wanting to change the world.

By the early 1990s, our work in London had inspired

other branches of People First to start up in other cities. My work took me to a UN panel in Toronto where I spoke in front of 1,800 people about disability rights. I presented a documentary series, *Life of Our Own*, for the BBC. It was about the ordinary lives of people with learning disabilities, showing us doing everything from using public transport to cooking and going out with friends. I wanted to change perceptions and I was aware I was doing something different. I had big dreams, all this energy and vision about what I wanted to see happen. I was buzzing.

When you've got a dream and vision and your heart's set on achieving something, then having the right support around you is vital. Money's helpful, but success to me involves making things happen with the help of a good network. I've had that through most of my working life. We all need people to encourage our vision. It's the opposite of me wanting to do chemistry at school, and being told 'no'. It should be, 'Let's see how we can do this.'

Because I've achieved things, people might think I'm immortal or indestructible. But I'm not. I'm only human like everyone else, and I need and like to have someone to support me. To be successful, you need someone who believes in you and who you can learn from and go to if there's a crisis. You need someone to bounce ideas off, and you find out pretty quickly who you're good at working with.

I was in my twenties and only just gaining my confidence when I met John, and he helped me to build on that. With John's friendship, I became more assertive and developed my self-esteem. He'd help me with rehearsing my speeches – preparation is key in public speaking. John was easy to talk to and he was a good listener, and he still is. He treated me like a human being and had a big influence on me. He's a good guy, and this is what he has to say about me:

People usually talk based on their own experience, and that's as far as it goes. But the thing about Gary is that he's always been able to put things into words and then place those words in a bigger context so what he says feels relevant to more people. Gary's also talked in soundbites and slogans right from the start.

He became the leader of the self-advocacy groups I supported in the 1980s because of how he spoke and because of what he had to say. He was unhappy at how the day centres for people with learning disabilities were run, but in public he'd contain his anger and speak calmly. Sure, his jaw tightened and he would say his piece – but he never lost it, because after a while people stop listening.

Gary was also always very generous in supporting others. At meetings, some people could be very nervous speaking publicly, visibly shaking, and Gary would go and stand by their side and just say, 'Go on, that's all right.' He just stood there giving them moral support, that was just something he did instinctively; it was a very natural, incredibly powerful image.

The campaigning that Gary was leading was the early stages of a new movement, but even at the time people were talking about it as the last civil rights movement – and Gary was one of those civil rights leaders. That's what's fuelled him, the sense of injustice and the desire to improve people's lives.

John also told me about the City Literary Institute, an adult education college in central London where he ran classes in self-advocacy and writing. City Lit, as it's known, had a reputation as a radical place, with loads of different courses for people with learning disabilities. It was an exciting time to be there. I studied playwriting, theatre, photography and art. I made friends there that I still have now and I met one of my girlfriends there. Students with learning disabilities were treated with respect – it was such a big contrast to what I'd had at the residential school and day centre. We were treated as adults, as students no different from any others. I discovered that when I learned new things, my confidence grew and the theatre and playwriting helped me with my public speaking.

It was amazing when City Lit awarded me a lifetime fellowship. It's something that's given to people with a connection to the college who have had a positive impact on educating adults in the UK.

Success is about having freedom and being able to choose the support you need. That might be help with things like washing or dressing or it might just be some extra help with paying bills. It's about the right to choose who supports you and how. Everyone's different. The most important thing is to be independent. To be your own boss.

I feel successful when I'm meeting people and telling them my story or promoting my ideas – and then I get that 'wow' factor from them. I've had people come up to me at conferences and say I've inspired them. I've been told I'm a role model for other people. It's amazing to hear, but I don't see it so easily myself. I need to ask people sometimes, 'How did I do?' and, 'How did I come across?' I still ask this even after all this time, because I can't judge it sometimes. I'm too busy doing it to think about how I did it.

My advice for younger people who want to do what I do would be to go to college, learn as much as you can, mix with other students and go on leadership courses. But there's nothing in our schools to support that. There's no proper professional careers advice. You might get a well-meaning teacher here and there, but no one with formal training to help achieve what you want to do in life. Without this, people's dreams are dampened down.

I want people to have not just a job but also a career. Not everyone with a learning disability wants to work in a supermarket, but jobs for learning-disabled people aren't ever talked about in terms of professions. If they were, it could change how everyone sees us. I've always thought that more people could set up their own businesses too – self-employment shouldn't be ruled out. Just because it's not a traditional option for learning-disabled people doesn't mean it's not an option. We could do with more supported employment, which is when you have help from people like job coaches who guide and settle you into the new work. There are some great examples of this around the country, but it's a postcode lottery. Whether or not you get it depends on where you live.

The government wants to get more disabled people into work but they put obstacles in our way to get there, like cutting benefits that help us stay more independent. Politicians get upset if they don't get the grey vote, the black and minority ethnic vote or the youth vote. They worry about all those figures, but when it comes to people with a learning disability, it's not an area they worry about. The challenge is convincing politicians that people have got a lot to contribute to society, to the economy and to making life better generally. We need to visit places like Harrow and Eton and do disability awareness training, because a lot of future politicians will come from these schools.

I want to see people having better lives and better health and care in the community, not in big institutions. In 2011, the BBC programme *Panorama* exposed the abuse of people with learning disabilities at Winterbourne View, the private hospital in South Gloucestershire, and there are still thousands of learning-disabled people locked away in places like that, these secure units, even though the government promised to close them all down and move people back home. They should never have been allowed to exist in the first place, but the fact they're still here is worrying. It says something about the way our society views learning-disabled people. These units are very expensive to run, and that money would be better spent providing housing and well-trained staff to allow the people that live there to be properly supported to live in the community.

Part of the problem is that people with learning disabilities aren't involved in creating the kind of support that helps them. You need their input to plan and develop services, working alongside non-disabled people. Then there's a better chance the service you're developing will meet the needs of the people who are going to use it. People are more likely to want to use it if they know other learning-disabled people have helped to create it.

I hope that the younger generation coming through now will carry on the good work we've done so far. We need strong leaders for the future, to represent people with learning disabilities and to carry on the learning disability civil rights movement. Young people with learning disabilities should have aspirations, but you don't hear people talk about what they could go on to achieve. People need to see their future. Mrs Elgar's school is still going; I'd love to go back and meet the children who go there today. What a story I could tell them.

I just want to see disabled people doing ordinary things. That's our society: a multicultural, multi-ability society. You've got to have ambition and a vision and a dream. You don't want people to rubbish your dream. It doesn't matter that somebody will say, 'This is unachievable.' It's important to have something you want to make happen – it's important to have an idea. I am ambitious. Be ambitious.

———————————————

Gary Bourlet is a veteran civil rights campaigner who founded Learning Disability England in 2016. The campaigning membership group is the first organisation to bring together people with learning disabilities, their families, friends and care professionals in a common cause. In 1984 he launched the international disability civil rights movement People First in the UK, and over the last thirty years has set up campaign groups all over the country, training people with learning disabilities in leadership roles and encouraging them to speak up for themselves. In 2018 Gary was awarded a lifetime fellowship at the City Literary Institute in London.

@BourletGary

Loud and Proud

Lizzie Emeh

I'd like to start where it all began. It began with me hearing music in a totally different way. I was born and bred in Notting Hill, west London, with the Notting Hill Carnival right on my doorstep. My childhood was spent surrounded by music, but my hearing wasn't great (in fact, in 2011 I was diagnosed as deaf). So I *felt* the music from the carnival; I heard the vibration and the beat, and I'd sing and dance in the street.

Being brought up in an Irish-Nigerian household, there was always a diverse range of music being played. We had folk, reggae and Afrobeat, but also Duran Duran and the Dubliners. My late mum taught me about the blues. She introduced me to soul – from Aretha Franklin to Otis Redding to Sam Cooke. Mum would play old Motown records – she had so much vinyl. Did you know vinyl sounds much more clear than music recorded on anything else? More clear than cassettes or CDs. I used to hear it crystal clear when it was played loud. There's something about touching the vinyl – the warmth of vinyl and the sound – and then you put on the needle ever so gently. Just getting the record out of the sleeve is a special thing.

I used to watch the singers my parents liked on video and be captivated by them all. I loved the way James Brown or Otis Redding controlled the stage. My late dad thought I watched too many music videos so he used to try and distract me, but Mum would say, 'Leave her.' My dad didn't realise that for me, listening to music and watching people perform was an education (he came to realise this, but that's when he was much older).

I have two brothers and a sister, and I'm the youngest. When I was born, doctors told my parents that I wouldn't ever be able to walk, talk or sit up. I knew I was different from the word go. My mum dismissed it; she was like, 'You're no different to your sister or your brothers, you're just special.' I remember my mum teaching me to speak. She would hold a ball and say, 'B-a-l-l,' or point to a table and say, 'T-a-b-l-e.' I remember thinking, 'You're totally cuckoo! Of course I know what they are!'

My dad would say, 'She'll talk in her own time.' And that's what I did. My very first word when I was about four was my brother's name, Christopher. I called to him from downstairs, and he flew down the stairs, yelling, 'She said my name, Mum! Mum!'

One day, when I was seven or eight, I was in the bath and my mum was singing a 1980s a cappella song, 'Only You' by the Flying Pickets. I joined in. Mum turned round and said, 'I'm going to do something with you, with this – I'm gonna take you to Ireland, to your nan in Dublin.' My nan was an amateur jazz and blues singer, so Mum took me home to Ireland and said to my nan, 'She's got this wicked gift, what shall I do with it?' Nan said, 'Leave her with me for a year. I will teach her everything she needs to know.'

My nan taught me about music and she was the most inspirational person in my life. She made me want to be a singer. She went through this A to Z of music with me. She used to sing different songs in different ways, Irish music as well as folk and jazz like Ella Fitzgerald. She would sing, oh man, she would sing! Nan sang with me all the time, she gave me the passion. She would get me to harmonise with her. No one else in my family sings – it's only me who has that gift. It's definitely come straight from my nan – she was so soulful. It missed a generation because my mum couldn't sing a blind note, but one of my brothers and my sister are musical too. My sister played the violin at school and my brother used to like singing.

If Nan hadn't had the wagonload of kids that she did (she had twenty-three kids!), she would have sung professionally. She was offered a record deal but she had her kids to look after. Instead, she sang in clubs, at parties, funerals; she was singing all of the time. She was all about the razzmatazz. When the whole family got together at my nan's on a Saturday night, it was showtime. 'It's your turn – what can you do?' she would ask us kids. There was singing, dancing and poetry. My nan just opened up the floor to us. At Nan's, it was escapism and freedom. I really felt like I could express myself. When I moved back home to London from Ireland, my nan spoke to my mum about how I loved the music. 'She needs to hear it full blast,' she said. 'Don't put it on low for Liz.' I remember my nan turning around to me and saying, 'I'm only putting you on the starting blocks, because I know what you're going to achieve.'

I have had difficult times. When I was around nine or ten, I would play outside with some other kids who lived nearby. My mum kept saying, 'Why do you keep on calling these your mates? They're not your friends, Liz. They put dog mess into a tissue and wipe it all over you – is that what you call a friend?' I said, 'It's not done on purpose,' because I wanted friends. When my mum went outside and began screaming at them because of what they'd done to me, my dad said, 'Come in, you're making a show of yourself, why are you wasting your time?' Mum said they shouldn't get away with it, but Dad said her going and shouting her head off was not going to achieve anything. He said she was wasting her breath because they needed an education.

Here is something that happened a few years ago. I am walking down the road with my nephew, and this boy he knows comes up and asks, 'Why does your aunty walk funny – are her feet on back to front?' The minute he says that, my nephew starts on him, trying to kick him, and I am screaming at him to stop, and he says, 'Aunty Liz, they shouldn't get away with that.' Later, my mum sits him down and talks to him. She says, 'Your Aunty Liz, she is very, very special. Do you know why? Because she has got disabilities and you have got to educate people about that.' He says,

'That's impossible, because people aren't going to listen.' And she says, 'Screaming and shouting ain't going to make any difference.' So my mum had changed her mind about how to deal with these people over the years.

Here is another story. I'm on the bus and this young lad turns round and says to his sister, 'Now *that* is what I call a retard.' They both start laughing. But then this voice comes from the back of the bus and says – I don't know who it was, but it was brilliant – 'If she's a retard, you're the one that needs an education.' A lot of people need an education about learning disability. I want people to respect us. There are people who say stupid things. Like the time someone said, 'The freaks are out on patrol,' when I was out clubbing with some mates.

I agree with my dad on this: it's not about confrontation, it's about education. That's what I'm doing now by just getting out there and singing. My God, that's making a bigger difference than shouting.

Also, what these people don't understand is that what they say gives me lyrics for my songs, and then I write about how stupid people are. This shows them up. So what I would say to them is, 'The more that you say silly stuff to me, the more you are giving me material – so yeah, go on, please say stupid stuff to me because then the laugh's on you, not me.' One of my songs, 'People Over the World', includes the line, 'I don't like people laughing at me, why do they have to do that? It hurts inside.' I like to write about people who are ignorant about learning disabilities. I called my debut album *Loud and Proud* because I wanted to be celebratory about learning disability.

Why have we got these attitudes? It's because of the way that people with learning disabilities used to be treated years ago, going way back to when they were locked up or hidden away in day centres and stuff like that. So people used to make fun of them.

Every single song that I write has a message. 'Loud and Proud' is a tune that says people shouldn't be put off by the barriers that are put in their way. The song 'See Me' is about the death of my mother. The song is about the fact you have to try and be positive, which is what Mum would have wanted for me. I wrote it about how you mustn't be sad when people leave you because they would want you to be happy.

Another track, 'Pills', is about the medication I'm on for my mental health (I have bipolar disorder). The right medication can help, so it's about not letting the pills control you – you control the pills. I have written about this too. So my own experiences really influence what I put into the lyrics. The EP trilogy I finished in 2019 (the first two parts came out in 2015 and 2016) is based on what I've been through. The different songs tell people about my mental health experiences and dealing with hearing loss.

I write true stories, I write true songs, funny stuff about my background, and I sing from the heart about life. My music is raw. I say it how it is. I've written about my mum and dad arguing, and the next-door neighbour would be like, 'The Emeh family's at it again.' My dad used to say it was a 'big *wahala*' – *wahala* is Nigerian slang for problem.

Extract from 'Loud and Proud', co-written with Mark Williams

You and your stupid language.
We do what we want,
We do what we like,
In our own time.
Some people say that we are mad,
Some people say that we are sad,
All we think about is confrontation,
How about recommendation?

Extract from 'See Me', co-written with Arthur Lea

She wants me to be happy inside.
No more sadness inside.
She wants me to carry on so the sun will still shine on.

Extract from 'Pills', co-written with Rikki Jodelko

Those pills are rattling and shaking all over me.
My pills are rattling and shaking all over me.
… Don't let the pills control you, you control the pills.

I write or co-write all my songs, and when we write and record, we just go at a slower pace than some musicians (my album *Loud and Proud* took three years to produce). How I write is that I hear the beat first – the drums – then I get the lyrics in my head. Then I work with other musicians to come up with the melodies. I know how the song should sound in my head and I explain what I want the musicians to do. I just pass on what I need everyone to play through singing the tune. My co-writers transcribe my words and help me get across the mood I am after.

So, say we're in the studio and I've got an idea for the song. The first thing I might do is ask the guitarists for a wah-wah bass and a choppy bass. I'd maybe ask for a reggae-style keyboard, a ska drumbeat and maybe reggae percussion. I'd work out what backing vocals we need – something a bit ska, maybe – and the horn section gets going. Then I jump in with the lyrics.

Once we've laid down the track, I might listen back to it and think, *Yeah, something's missing here*, like we need more horns, so I'll say to the horn players, 'I wonder if you could do this, "da da daaa daa daaaah".' And they do it.

When I write, I love writing for the horn section – like the sax or trumpet. It brings out my jazz and blues side. My favourite instruments in the whole wide world are horns. I love live horns. When I hear the horns on stage something just happens inside me – I don't know – I just totally feel the sound. Horns need to be played loud. Once the track sounds like it did in my head, then it's done. I describe my music as eclectic, wide-ranging and with lots of soul.

I work with some incredible musicians. There's Charles Stuart, who tours with Grace Jones, and Robbie Fordjour, a drummer for Courtney Pine. The session musicians I collaborate with are amazing; my trumpeter Rory Simmons has worked with Blur, Paolo Nutini and Jamie Cullum. For the horn section, we get Trevor Miles on trombone – he's played with Tom Jones – and George Crowley on sax; he's worked with Boy George. J. B. Rose is my vocal trainer and does background vocals at my live performances and on my EPs. She's also a singer-songwriter.

When you're collaborating in the studio, you might start with one kind of vibe – like the cocktail-lounge thing – and then you vibe off each other and it all gets a bit more funky. I love going into the studio. I love performing too, but when I go into the studio that is when the magic happens. I absolutely adore it.

Everyone I work with brings something different. With Charles Stuart, for example, he brings out my sensitive side. By the time we finish the song, I'm in floods of tears because it's so moving what he can do with a tune. One of the tracks I did with Charles, 'Come Into the Light', is about my brothers. The message is if you need me, I'm here. We recorded it with musicians from the London Symphony Orchestra and the strings are just beautiful.

I wouldn't be doing what I do without the arts organisation Heart n Soul. Without it, I would not have had the chance to perform. Heart n Soul also gives me advice, arranges my vocal training, songwriting sessions and coordinates my rehearsals and gigs. It also gets the word out there about what I do. I have someone who does my marketing campaigns and press work, and they run my website for me. Heart n Soul's basically helped me develop the Lizzie Emeh 'brand'. Through the charity I also have someone who helps me keep on top of what they call 'wellbeing'. That's about making sure my health's OK and I'm feeling good, eating well, that kind of thing. It's basically like having a really good mate who I can talk to about stuff and who keeps an eye out for me.

The way I see it, my mum spotted my gift and my nan grew it. But when Heart n Soul entered my life – or I entered Heart n Soul's life! – it was like I went through a magic door.

I made a very important decision when I was about twenty-one. I went to a club night in south-east London organised by Heart n Soul and tried the open-mic session. I was there with Colin, a care worker who was with me at the time (I live in supported housing, so I have my own place, but I have care workers to help me with stuff). He knew I sang and said, 'You see everyone up there doing their thing? Why don't you have a go? Just try?' So I went up and did Tracy Chapman's 'Talkin' 'Bout a Revolution'. Before I'd even got to the end of the track, I saw Mark Williams, the artistic director of Heart n Soul, at the foot of the stage. As soon as I came off, Mark said, 'I would like you to come for an audition with Heart n Soul so we can represent you as a singer.'

Like Colin said then, 'It's now or never,' so the next week I went to the audition. It could have gone badly wrong because two days before, I was making my bed and lifted it – and dropped it down right onto my foot. It's a cast-iron bed, so it broke my foot – but I still did the audition on crutches!

Singing at that open-mic night and then at the audition, it was the first time I felt like I didn't have a disability. Heart n Soul loved what I did and asked me to come back and work with them. I've never told Mark this, but I honestly think he saved my life. He really believed in what I could do. He's the one who said, 'You know what? You can do it. Come on, why not take the gamble?' Mark was 100 per cent behind me five years later when I said I wanted to make an album. He has a way of building confidence in people, which is very special. To this day I'm extremely thankful – I'm not sure he really knows how much he changed my life.

When I'm on stage, it makes me feel proud that I'm there, like I'm saying, 'Look what I can do and what I've done so far.' But I'm not doing this for myself: I want to do it for people with disabilities. When I know that I have changed how people think about people like me, or something I have sung has made a difference to someone, that makes me feel like I've achieved something. A friend told me that my track 'Pills', about mental health, is very important to someone she knows who has bipolar disorder. She told me it made perfect sense about how to handle it. To know that I've helped someone else, and I'm changing people's attitudes, that's the achievement. When you come off stage and someone turns around and says, 'That really touched me,' you know that what you're talking about is true, and it's real life.

My biggest moment performing was at the opening ceremony of the London 2012 Paralympics. I did 'Loud and Proud' in front of 80,000 people and I accompanied Beverley Knight, who sang Gloria Gaynor's 'I Am What I Am'. It was an amazing feeling. And of course I'm so proud to be the first solo artist with a learning disability to release an album of my own songs to the UK public.

You know what, though, marriage is one of my biggest achievements. I got married in 2016 and I wrote 'Waiting' about my husband, Eddie. I met Ed through a mutual friend. When I first met him, he looked at me in a way that was like, 'Yeah, I'm gonna have you.' I felt it too. There was a chemistry between us, but I was with someone else back then so we didn't do anything about it. Eventually it did not work out with my boyfriend, so about six years after that first meeting, I said to Eddie, 'Do you fancy going out with me?' He looked around and joked, 'Who me? You're joking!' He ran around like he'd won the lottery or something. We took it slowly, to get to know each other. Then one day in 2012, nearly a year after my mum had died, he said – very casually – 'Liz, what would happen if we got married?' He was extremely relaxed. He didn't go on one knee or anything. I said, 'Are you asking me?' He said, 'Yeah, would you?' I said yes, of course.

I do remember that when we started talking about marriage, there were a few people – friends who have learning disabilities, staff that worked with Eddie – who said, 'You're off your heads – how's that going to work?' First I worried people were laughing at us. Then I thought that maybe they were being negative about us getting married because they were trying to protect us – but from what? Attitudes I suppose, because a lot of people maybe don't expect people like me to get married. But I said to Eddie, 'Let's prove them wrong.' Why should it be any different for people with learning disabilities to get married? We're human beings – we're just special that's all.

We were married at a registry office in south-east London. It took us a very long time to arrange the wedding, and for us to be content and happy about how the day would be. It had to be just right. Our carers made it possible so we had no stress.

My dress was plain white, with a plain white jacket. I wanted to reflect my Irish heritage, so my bridesmaids were in green. Ed went all traditional. He had this simple, suave, sophisticated suit and a white shirt. The flowers were white and yellow and my friend's mum arranged all the flowers. One of my carers decorated the hall – it looked amazing. Eddie wanted to show a bit of his family's heritage too. His dad was a bus conductor, so we had an old Routemaster bus from the register office to the reception at a hotel.

All my musicians came to the wedding. The guy who gave me away was Rikki, my guitarist. Mark Williams was there, Arthur was there, Robbie was there, J. B. was there. My band played and I sang. The entertainment was easily sorted – and free! The honeymoon suite at the hotel was something else. There were rose petals on the bed, swans made out of towels and they were arranged on the bed as if they were kissing. Ed and I, oh Lord, we tried to move these swans and they absolutely fell apart! We were just falling about laughing.

I always thought I was going to get married. I knew a Prince Charming would come along! Ed is one of my biggest fans – he's always at the front at my gigs. It feels really amazing when I see him in the audience. I feel really happy, and if I don't see him, I feel insecure. It is like he is my safety guard. He gets what I do too, because he used to be a rigger, helping set up the equipment for gigs. He's definitely The One, and I want to share my life with him.

There's this game I love playing with people, because I always win hands down. You ask someone, 'Who's the most famous person you've ever met?' No one can beat me, and I think my answer shows how successful I've been. Because I met Nelson Mandela. I met him through the Diana, Princess of Wales Memorial Fund, which, until it closed in 2012, used to support Heart n Soul. One of the perks of that was meeting the great man himself. When Mark told me I was going to meet him, my knees just turned to jelly and I dropped to the floor. 'What do I say?' I asked Mark. 'Hello would be a good start,' he joked. I met him in 2002 at Althorp House, the family home of Princess Diana. Earl Spencer, Diana's brother, and this frail old gentleman walked in. He said to me, 'It is an honour and a privilege to meet you.' In my head, I was saying, *That's the opposite way around, surely?*

Meeting Mandela was such a significant moment in my life. I remember I was thirteen years old when I heard he had been freed from prison. I went to the Notting Hill Carnival with my mum not long after, and everyone was shouting and screaming his name. So it was an incredible moment to meet him. There is a photograph of me with Mandela, and my dad took it back to Nigeria to show the relatives. After I met Mandela, it was like my dad accepted me as someone who really knew what she was doing.

There was a time, you see, when Dad wasn't so certain about my preferred career plans. He worried people might take advantage of me because of my disabilities and said the industry would rip me to shreds. Just after I released my first album, Dad was in hospital for a routine operation and he saw me on the television they had on in his ward. I was being interviewed on the local London news about how we made the album, and they showed one of my music videos. He just couldn't believe it. I think he realised then that I was successful. My mum said to him, 'I told you what she could do,' and my dad just kept saying to the nurses, 'That's my daughter, that's my daughter!' Dad knew I could sing – he encouraged me to strive and told me not to give up – but it was only when he saw me on television that I think it sank in and he saw what I could do. Dad was so proud of me.

The reason I'm here, the reason I am successful, is my voice and my music. When I am on stage, I do not have a disability. I come alive on stage, like someone's plugged me into the mains. My music is really different because you can have me as the big jazz-hands thing with a big band, or I can put together a down-tempo five-piece outfit. I'm in control of the band, and the musicians follow my lead.

My aim is to get the audience feeling the same vibe we feel on stage. I think what people are attracted to is not just my music; it's also how I communicate with the audience. I love the interactions that I have with the band on stage. I like bouncing from the band to the audience and back. I feel like I have that extra bounce that whips things up on stage. That comes from my nan, because she taught me how to build up during a performance. It's amazing to hear the audience shouting or singing along to my tracks – to actually hear them calling for a song that I have written. I remember doing a gig and just before I went on, I could hear the audience, and everyone was waving their hands and shouting, 'Loud and proud… c'mon we're loud and proud!' When I'm performing and people sing my lyrics back to me, it's a weird feeling that they know my songs, but it feels really good.

My success is also because I've got the right people around me and they're people I trust. It's also about my look and, of course, my music – I'm the full package. Because I've been working with Heart n Soul for over fifteen years, we've had lots of time to come up with my look. I love it when we are doing a photoshoot and I get to show my Nigerian side. I love the head wraps that I wear and the clothes. I wear a lot of bold colours, like reds and purples, and I am a big fan of prints. I'm so blessed that Mark takes such care in everything we do. I might turn round and say to him, 'What do you think about this look, or this hair?' and he just says, 'Whatever you want.' So I call the shots; I am not controlled. Let the people work for you, I always say, you don't work for them.

Music has always been the way for me. Everything that you hear from me is my own music, my own creation. If I wasn't doing my music, I'd be sat at home doing nothing and being bored.

I'm successful because I have a certain standard that I operate at. I love Amy Winehouse; she wrote from the heart, she sang about really personal things, but she didn't get enough care, support or love – it was just work, work, work. My favourite Amy Winehouse song is 'You Know I'm No Good'. But Stevie Wonder is the biggest icon in my life. Oh my, I saw him live a few years ago in London. Everyone was screaming, hollering and howling, and I was just blabbering on about how amazing he was, and all I could do was dance. 'Master Blaster' is my favourite track and my dream duet would be with Stevie Wonder, oh yeah. Or Adele – she's a big inspiration. That's the professional level I aim for. I spend a lot of time rehearsing, even if I have a hospital appointment or I'm feeling a bit under the weather. Do you honestly think Beverley Knight has a day off? Unless I'm really, seriously ill, I don't want to take time out. If I'm fit and able to do it, I do it.

I want to get more people to do what I've done. I want more people to be able to find their own magical door and see that stuff is possible. I want to inspire other people with disabilities so they can say, 'If she can do that, so can we.' People with disabilities are always told what they cannot do. I want to change that. When I came across Heart n Soul, no one cared about my disability. They were just interested in my raw talent. My ambition is all about education, education, education. It is not about the fame or the money. I want to be known for my music, but the more important achievement is that I'm changing people's attitudes. I used to say I want a MOBO Award, but the biggest award for me would be for more people to understand more about learning disability. I want people to see me as a person with no limits and no barriers and see me for the talent that I have and what I can do with it.

To help make this happen, I think there should be lots more arts organisations like Heart n Soul in other parts of the country. A few of my mates can't travel far, and they say, 'You know what, Liz, we are missing out on what you do – why ain't there another thing like this where we live?' I tell them, 'Give me a few years to work on that; I'd love to have a Lizzie Emeh school for arts.' But my performing arts school would be for people with disabilities and for people without disabilities. We also need to educate the music industry, so it's more open to artists like me. It's a great thing to have different perspectives and experiences in the arts.

If there are people out there who want to do what I do, I'd say don't ever, ever give up on your dreams. Don't ever give up on what's inside you. Always try and prove people wrong. Doctors, teachers, anyone who tells you all that you can't do stuff. If you want to be a singer like me, be true to yourself, be true to your fans and write whatever is true to you. Then you've got a recipe for success.

Lizzie Emeh launched her debut album *Loud and Proud* in 2009, making history as the first solo artist with a learning disability to release an album of her own songs to the public. In 2012 Lizzie performed at the London Paralympic Games opening ceremony with Beverley Knight. She has also played Glastonbury and performs regularly at the Royal Festival Hall with Heart n Soul, the London-based arts organisation that produces her music. Lizzie released *Meds*, the final EP in her autobiographical EP trilogy *See Me*, in 2019. She is always working on new music.

If in Doubt, Balls Out

Dan Pepper

My disability has never stood in the way of my success. Everyone needs support to achieve their dreams, but the people supporting you mustn't try to do so much for you that they somehow take over. The most important thing is that you get to where you want to go yourself, your way.

I first got into swimming when I was four years old. It was purely for safety reasons, because our house in Stockport backed on to a canal and my parents were worried that my two sisters and I might fall in. All three of us learned to swim, but my sisters weren't into racing as hard as me. It was only me who progressed it and took it really seriously. Something just clicked into place in the pool, and I enjoyed going fast in the water. I was talent-spotted at a gala by my local swimming club and I started going to local competitions.

My natural instinct takes over in a race and I just want to win. I also succeed by being strict with myself because I always remember how I need to race. During my competitive swimming career, I never used to concentrate on anyone else but myself. My focus was on how I swam and my ultimate goal was to come first.

I remember the 2010 Swimming World Championships at Eindhoven in the Netherlands. The event was organised by the International Paralympic Committee and, apart from the Paralympics, it was the most important worldwide swimming event for competitors with disabilities. So there I am in the pool for the 200-metre freestyle, I turn at the end of the lane at 100 metres and I'm something like sixth in the race. Then I turn at 150 metres and, although I'm not looking round to check where the others are, I can only see one other swimmer ahead of me. I'm now second. I'm winning by a body length. I won gold for that race and also for the 100-metre breaststroke. But if I'd worried too early about where I was compared to the other swimmers, I'd have thought, *God, I'm miles behind.* I could have blown my engine too early. Winning is all about learning how to compete, how to pace yourself and staying calm under pressure.

Everyone feels differently when they race, whether that's a swim or a run. I'm naturally quite a relaxed guy, so when I compete I don't get nervous, maybe just a little anxious. Some people really get themselves fired up and others are so relaxed they are almost asleep. I'm somewhere between those two extremes. If I get too worked up then there's too much adrenalin and I don't race right.

When I was swimming at elite level, I'd stick to a pre-race routine to get me in the right frame of mind. I'd plug in my headphones first and listen to some music, usually some

R & B. I'd pull up the hood on my sweatshirt so I didn't get distracted, and that helped chill me out. Then I'd take off my shoes, then my tracksuit bottoms and then my top – in that exact same order every time – and I'd fold them carefully. In the couple of minutes before the race, I'd splash some pool water on myself, do a few strokes in the air and I'd always get onto the block from the side rather than from behind it. Having a familiar routine was reassuring; I felt in control. Doing the same thing before each race kept me focused.

I only swam three times a week until I was twelve, which is when I began swimming competitively. By the time I was a teenager I had a much more serious training regime. I'd be up at 4 a.m. five times a week. My parents would take me to the pool to train from 4.30 a.m. to 7.30 a.m., then they'd bring me back and I'd cycle to school. After school I'd bike home, do my homework, train in the pool again for three hours, come back, eat, and go to bed by 9.30 p.m. Rinse and repeat. I don't remember ever not wanting to go or it being a struggle to get up. My parents never pushed or forced me to do it, because I could see the results from training so hard.

On top of my pool training, I'd be in the gym four times a week and have regular sports massage and physio sessions. When I was preparing for the Paralympics, I'd be in the pool from 6 a.m. to 8 a.m, then in the gym until 10.30 a.m. and then back again in the pool from 3 p.m. to 5 p.m. I had a nutritionist who made sure I ate three well-balanced meals a day, and I'd be snacking on cereal bars or protein shakes after pool sessions, and I'd have to make sure I had 1.5 litres of water a day.

Inevitably, the training can get repetitive. So if you want to be successful, the key thing is to have a coach who makes it interesting and knows when to push you and when to back off a bit if you're having a bad day. I might get in the pool on a Monday morning and absolutely fly, and I might do that for four days on the trot, but then I might get in on the fifth day and just not feel right for whatever reason. That's not because I'm not trying, but just because that spark's not there at that particular moment. A coach who knows what they're doing will know when to take you out of the pool and make it easier, or tell you to get a grip. They know what makes you tick. A good coach understands you as a person and not just as a swimmer. Winning is as much about what's in your mind, how you feel mentally, as it is about physical skill.

I was first coached for success at my local club, Marple Swimming Club. The club saw my talent early on and encouraged me to join something called the Link Scheme, run by Stockport Metro, a much bigger, city-wide swimming club. The scheme means local club swimmers can take their competitive swimming to a higher level. After, that there was no turning back. I kept my membership at Marple but did all my training at Stockport Metro. When I began swimming in national and international championships, a coach called Mick Massey took me on and brought me up a gear.

Mick was a Team GB Paralympic coach and he's an absolutely crucial part of my success. He coached me as a twelve-year-old novice all the way to become a world champion. Mick always kept me positive; he knew when to push me to the max and also when to give me space. He'd make me do breaststroke with sponges attached to me on ropes, so they'd absorb water as I'd drag them through the pool. I'd be completely broken at the end of the session, but he'd be larking about, pointing at the sponges around me saying, 'Oh, you've caught three haddock, two cod and a carp!' No matter how shattered I felt, he'd make me laugh.

Mick was the kind of coach who supports you professionally as well as on a more social, personal level. Even now, he's a friend I can lean on for advice. He'd do simple things that meant a lot, like take me for a quick bite to eat after training, just to a local noodle bar or a café. We'd hang out and I got to know Mick and his family really well. I became good friends with his daughter Natalie, who was also a Paralympic swimmer with Team GB, and we ended up going out. We're married now and I never get tired of joking with Mick that even though he's no longer my coach he can't get rid of me because I'm part of the family!

The former Olympic swimmer Steve Parry is another mentor who made a big difference to my career. Steve made training fun so we'd have a laugh in our pool sessions. That's not always easy to do when you have to be in the pool by 5 a.m.! He used to mix up his training with banter. Steve would challenge me to beat my lap time, or to be quicker off the starting block. He'd say the incentive to hitting my target was that he'd do the 200-metre butterfly, so I could see him bust a gut too. Butterfly is the most difficult in terms of technique and having the sheer muscle power to propel you through the water. Steve made sure I enjoyed training as much as I enjoyed the actual racing.

That idea of turning training sessions into a game or a challenge is something I've used in my own coaching, both in the pool and on land. When I teach kids to swim, the most important thing is that they have fun in the water and enjoy their sessions with me. With my personal fitness clients, part of keeping people motivated is making sure they enjoy their time with me and we have a laugh.

Learning disability affects people in different ways. I struggle with reading, writing and numbers. The counting can be a problem when I'm training because I find it hard to keep track of lengths and read the time on the clock. When I'd swim a medley race (which is when you use four swimming styles – butterfly, breaststroke, backstroke and freestyle), I'd sometimes struggle to remember which stroke I was meant to be doing.

But my disability hasn't stopped me being a successful athlete; it's just meant that I've had a different approach to success. I have coping strategies that help me make sure I'm not struggling. One thing that helps is good time management, because I get stressed unless I have plenty of time to get to the venue and get my head around the space where I'll be swimming. Simple adjustments can make all the difference. For example, a 200-metre swim on a short course, which is 25 metres long, is eight lengths, but on a long course of 50 metres it's four lengths. It can be very confusing! When I was training, my coaches made easy-to-read tables explaining the distances and how many lengths

I had to do. We'd stick this by the side of the pool and it helped me concentrate on my race, remember how many lengths to do and not feel anxious about the swim.

Sport has been incredibly important in my life. It's given me a lot more than just a physical skill in the pool. I went to the local primary and secondary schools, which is something my parents pushed for. The local education authority suggested special schools, but my parents were determined that all three of their kids had the same kind of education. I wasn't great academically, and I had a few lessons like maths and English in the special needs department, but if you got me in the pool I'd beat everyone.

Because I could swim and I looked like a strong lad, I was always respected. I was quicker than the other kids in PE and I thrived at sports days. I had a bit of name-calling from a few of the hard kids at school. I think it was down to me not being very good at academic subjects and wearing glasses (which weren't very fashionable). It made me even more determined to show people what I could do and be grateful for the support and backing my friends gave me. The name-calling was mainly from the lads who did football (which wasn't my sport), but I didn't get anything worse than that. I made some good friends at school and I felt that in some ways my swimming compensated for my disability.

I did my first international race when I was thirteen years old. It was in Hong Kong, in term time, and I was representing Great Britain at the INAS World Championships (INAS is the International Federation for Athletes with Intellectual Impairments). I won gold medals in the 100-metre and 200-metre breaststroke events and I knew some of the kids back home would be watching the livestream and seeing me take two gold medals. It made me feel proud that I was doing something that no one else at my school could do. My learning support teacher recorded the event to show to my form and the staff. When I got back from Hong Kong I took my medals into assembly and everyone made a big fuss of me. This was a bit embarrassing at the time, but something I now look back on with pride.

When you're in a good sports club, a club where you feel at ease, then it feels more like a family than anything else. That's how I felt at the two swimming clubs I belonged to, Marple and Stockport Metro. Sometimes I felt like I was getting out of bed at 4 a.m. and training from 4.30 a.m. more because I didn't want to let the rest of the club down rather than actually wanting to improve my strokes. You can't beat that team spirit. I'd be less keen to push myself in my work and everything else without the sport.

Being an athlete also means I have to be organised and on time. I have to be on top of stuff like making sure my kit bag's in order, working out a training regime or figuring out the logistics for getting to and from a venue. Swimming's also taught me a general respect and courtesy for my teammates and coaches. More than anything, it's kept me motivated to succeed and go from one goal to the next.

Without swimming I wouldn't be so healthy and – let's be honest – you get a really good body from working out.

As a competitive swimmer I had absolutely rock-hard abs, muscular arms and strong shoulders. I'm still fit now, but when I was an elite athlete, I was totally ripped!

There's the social side as well; sport gives me loads of confidence because I feel good about myself. I've always got something in reserve that I can say to people when they say, 'So, what are you up to?' I've got something that others don't. I also think it releases the endorphins so it impacts on my mental health and state of mind. I feel instantly better with exercise, and the feeling when you've won a race or beaten a time is incredible.

What would my life be like without swimming? I genuinely don't know what I'd have done if I hadn't had this in my life. Oh man – I can't imagine it. I think I'd be like a couch potato and I'd be really shy. I wouldn't have met my wife or formed the friendships I've got now.

I've won more than forty gold, silver and bronze medals at the biggest European and international swimming competitions for athletes with disabilities. But my first wins as a child were at the Mini Meet Grand Prix, a series of swimming competitions that are held in Stockport every year. When I was at school I swam for my county, Cheshire, in the English Schools Swimming Association national competitions, then went on to swim for Great Britain as a teenager at different European and international championships.

One of my greatest achievements was when I became double world champion in 2010 after winning gold for both 100-metre breaststroke and 200-metre freestyle at the International Paralympic Committee Swimming World Championships in Eindhoven.

Competing in the Paralympics was my ultimate dream – but it almost didn't happen. There was a scandal after the Sydney 2000 games because the Spanish basketball team cheated by fielding ineligible players. The basketball team said they had learning disabilities when they didn't – they'd faked their disabilities. So officials at the Olympics banned all athletes with learning disabilities from all international competitions.

I still get angry thinking about the ban. It was like we were all discriminated against even though we'd done nothing wrong. I was so disheartened and let down that I quit swimming, even though I'd qualified for the Paralympic team. I felt like all those years of work were for nothing. It was a really upsetting time and I stayed out of the pool for about a month – the longest I've ever been without swimming – before my coach persuaded me to get back in. If I'm honest, I missed that feelgood factor of working hard and feeling fit.

For the London 2012 Paralympic Games, it was decided that swimmers with learning disabilities could compete again. I qualified for the 200-metre freestyle and 100-metre breaststroke events, so I finally got my dream of competing in the Games. But it was some years later than I'd hoped to, as I'd first qualified for Athens in 2004 and Beijing in 2008. In the heats I won the freestyle race and came third in the breaststroke, but ultimately I didn't win any medals.

The hardest thing in my competitive swimming career was the feeling that I missed out. The Paralympics was still an amazing experience, but I did feel frustrated and disappointed. I dealt with it by just cracking on.

I kept training and the following year I represented Great Britain again in Montreal, for the Swimming World Championships 2013. I won a silver medal in the 200-metre medley race. Looking back, although I didn't win a Paralympic medal, I do recognise what an incredible thing it was to have qualified for Team GB and to have had a place in that Olympic pool. I've got a London 2012 tattoo on my left arm, which I wanted done as a permanent reminder of the event. I wanted it to look nice, so I had it done in shades of grey (rather than colour) and the London 2012 writing is the same as on the original logo. It hurt when I had it done – but not so much that I bottled out! – and I wouldn't ever have it removed.

The race I'll never forget was the one in Montreal in 2013, my first big race after London 2012. I was in training for the event, but I had a cough and fever and I'd not been swimming right. It turned out I had a serious chest infection and I ended up in hospital for two weeks. Three days after being discharged I was on a plane to Canada, so I wasn't expecting much from the race because I was nowhere near my best.

So there I am at the side of the pool for the 200-metre individual medley. I want to race hard but I'm not sure my body's up to it. I do my usual routine with the hood, the headphones and the air strokes – but I feel like I need to get myself awake, so I chuck a bottle of ice-cold water over my head. I throw up straight away. Mick, my coach, says, 'Pull out the Pepper magic and see what happens.' He reckons I can pull a swim out of the bag and it suddenly hits me: this is it – this could be my last hurrah. I stand behind the block thinking, *Let's just give this a go.*

I feel strangely calm. I dive in and get through the butterfly; I keep my head down and focus on finishing the stroke rather than worrying about where I am compared to the other swimmers. I switch to backstroke and, I have no idea how this happens, but I swim the best 50 metres backstroke I've ever done in my life (it's my weakest stroke). I'm on the final stretch now and it's breaststroke – my best stroke – and freestyle (front crawl). I'm flying through the water and as I turn at the end of the pool I catch sight of Mick with his stopwatch. Mick – the usually placid Mick – is screaming and smiling and he throws down the stopwatch and I know I've done good. I just remember thinking, *I'm dead!* and Mick heaving me out of the water. I remember having a laugh with the other two swimmers who got medals, but I don't remember actually getting on the podium to get my silver. My best race. Ever.

There's definitely no way I could have achieved as much as I have without my family. My parents believed that I had skill and talent in the pool right from the start and they physically got me to and from those early-morning training sessions. It takes some commitment to drive your child around at that time! They supported me without being pushy parents, breathing down my neck and forcing me to succeed.

I remember one time when I had a competition in Sheffield; I wasn't expecting to do that well so I'd told them not to bother coming to watch. On the day I actually did really well in the heats and made it into the final race, so I rang to tell them. They totally floored it to Sheffield in the car after work and walked into the leisure centre just as I was getting on the starting block to dive in. They did a three-hour round trip to watch me swim for twenty-six seconds and win the race. I gave them a wave from the poolside and off they went home. It was a priceless moment and just typical of the effort they put into supporting me.

My parents always treated their three kids as individuals with their own talents and skills. I've got one older sister, Jo, and one younger sister, Jess. My family has always been amazing; they see me as Dan, not 'Dan with a disability'. My parents never compared me with my sisters or judged me against my sisters' successes. For my sisters, their personal bests would have been about things like school tests or being the local carnival queen; for me it was always the latest swim. In our family, whatever you did well was celebrated, regardless of anyone else's achievement. That philosophy affected how I was in the pool and has stayed with me to this day. I do what I do for myself, not because I want to prove anyone right or wrong.

I wouldn't have been able to develop my career if I wasn't married to someone who genuinely understands how important sport is to me. That's massively important. Natalie and I were mates before we began going out and what brought us together was our love of swimming and fitness. Our first wedding anniversary was in fact the same weekend as the Man vs Mountain challenge, an outdoor race in Snowdonia that involves running, swimming and abseiling. Natalie encouraged me to do it and celebrate our anniversary later, because she knew what it meant to me to compete in it.

I've also made lifelong mates through swimming and we'd hang out at each other's houses when we were kids. The friendships from then are the friendships I still have now. Both of my childhood swimming friends were groomsmen at our wedding. My mates don't have learning disabilities. I think some people think that all people with learning disabilities only go round with each other the whole time. That's a wrong assumption. It's sad, but that image is probably because of the fact that years ago people with learning disabilities were shoved into big group homes or in day centres. You just didn't see people out and about.

We need to change people's attitudes towards learning disability and we can do that through educating the public about it. A lot of people think you need to mollycoddle someone with a learning disability. So, say someone with a learning disability starts a new job, they might need to have a carer or supporter working alongside them for a few days while they settle in. But this means that their colleagues won't interact with them. It means they won't socialise with them. They need that support to kick things off, but other people need to realise they're still capable of doing good work on their own and they should get to know them.

I drive, I work, I have mates I go out with, Natalie and I get out together a lot, but a lot of people with learning disabilities don't get out much in the evenings. They might spend a few hours in a day centre and spend the whole evening at home alone. Sometimes I think care staff who work with people with learning disabilities run out of things to do with them.

Whether you have a disability or not, it's so important to have a strong support network if you want to succeed at something. You're never going to get anywhere if you don't have people encouraging and advising you. With parents, you want them to be supportive but not pushy. That doesn't mean your parents can't be disappointed for you if you've not done so well, but they need to be able to see you've given it your best shot.

When you have had a tough day, a challenging day, you need someone to listen to you. A strong team could be family, friends, teachers, coaches or managers. You need to let your team help you to reach your goals, and whoever's supporting you needs to know that you're trying to achieve your goals for yourself – not for them or anyone else. This was and is still a very important part of my career.

I want to show that people with learning disabilities can do a great job. That's why I'm proud to be an ambassador for My Sport, My Voice! The UK Sports Association for People with Learning Disability runs the ambassador project, and the aim is to highlight the talents of elite athletes who have learning disabilities. All the ambassadors have been chosen because we've excelled at what we do, and we want to inspire other people to take up sport and be successful at it.

I love being an ambassador. I want to try and give something back to sport because it's given me so much. My role is to raise awareness, challenge people's perceptions and show what people with learning disability can achieve. It's important to show what we can do not just within the sporting world, but also out there in society. I want the public to understand what we can do. We need to show ourselves off, in a way.

I do a lot of public speaking and I talk about what it takes to be an elite athlete. I've spoken at the House of Lords, at schools and at disability charities. I've spoken in front of more than 500 people at the School Games, a national competition involving all sorts of different sports that's led by the government's Department of Culture, Media and Sport. I like speaking in public. I don't plan it – it comes naturally and a lot of the time I'll sit there and listen to the rest of the speakers or the audience and pick up what they respond to and might be interested in hearing about. I'd definitely like to see a lot more disabled young people in sport. There's a feelgood factor you get from sport and fitness, and that's good for everyone – if you have a disability or not.

I really like the idea of helping young, upcoming athletes. One day I might work full time in that kind of coaching role, inspiring other people. I want to stay in swim coaching, but I want to be a coach for the coaches. I want to go to swimming clubs and see if their coaching methods actually work for someone with a learning disability. Generally, a physical difficulty is easier for people to get their heads round – it's harder for people to understand a learning disability. Sometimes it's not obvious that someone has a learning disability. Coaches need to see what someone might need to be adjusted. Some coaches might be scared and think they have to do a whole different training session for someone, but probably just one or two small tweaks – like me with my poolside chart – is all it would take.

One of the girls I coach at the swimming club has a learning disability. Let's call her Claire. When she first came, I wrote the training schedule on the board by the pool. I wrote down '200 free, 100 back', which means 200-metre freestyle, 100-metre backstroke, but I could see she didn't quite get it. Claire didn't understand that 200 is the same as eight lengths, and it reminded me of how I used to feel when I'd get confused about lengths. So I just wrote '8' on the board underneath '200'.

I didn't want to make her feel like she was different from the rest of the squad, so I spoke to them after her first session with us and asked everyone to be really welcoming. I explained that Claire had a learning disability so she'd be coming in with her mum, who'd show her around and help her settle in. I made it clear that she'd pick up the work we were doing, but that her induction might take two weeks whereas for them it took only one.

It's all about the communication and the benefits you gain from a short three-minute conversation. Such a small amount of time can make all the difference to someone like Claire. At the same time, I still expect Claire to do the eight lengths and put everything into it! I wasn't going to let her off with only six lengths or wrap her in cotton wool. As a coach, I have a structure to my training, but I can accommodate differences within that.

In my personal training business, I work with people who have learning disabilities and people who don't. Some people I work with are on medication for health or mental health problems that make them put on weight. Some people just want a personalised training programme and I help them work out what their goals are – to tone up, to feel fitter or to run faster. What I do totally depends on what the client wants. Sometimes I don't even meet my clients face to face but I do consultations on the phone or over email. I've done one-to-one sessions with someone with a learning disability who brought along her carer. One woman I trained went from not liking running to running on treadmill and taking herself to Park Run events. It was amazing to see her progress and to know I'd helped encourage that.

What I'd love is to open my own fitness centre for people of all abilities. Ideally, I'd have rooms where people can work out without being overlooked to encourage people who have a learning disability to try the gym – they know they won't they feel they're being stared at. It's important to stay well and look after yourself; it is about being healthy, not just fit.

If you're interested in sport, whether you're starting out or wanting to get to elite level, train hard, keep focused, remember why you're doing it but, above all, just enjoy it. If you don't enjoy it you're never going to reach your goal. Work hard, train and keep going. I'm not into the 'I can't do it' mentality.

I'm coaching a guy at the moment who is a regional champion and he is racing guys who train eight times a week. He's training five times a week, but he beats them because he enjoys it and when he's in the pool he thinks hard about what he's doing. We've got a phrase in our family: 'If in doubt, balls out.' It just means let's go for it, try your hardest and what's the worst that can happen? Give it a go – there's no reason not to try.

The other thing is to think about your next target. There's always the next competition to work towards and new goals to achieve; you can't just sit back and enjoy your latest success or you won't have any others. As much as I'm not swimming any more, there's so much I want to achieve. Every year I do a big endurance event like an Ironman Triathlon. I enter these big outdoor challenges because I'm aware that while I'm busy coaching and helping other people achieve their goals, I need to keep setting and reaching my own goals. Also, I find I can get a bit irritable if I don't work off some steam! Getting out makes me feel free, whether that's open-water swimming, biking, running or learning how to drive a speedboat (I did a powerboat course, which was awesome). I love the variety in my working life. One day I could be running a fitness boot camp, the next I'll be doing some swim coaching or training one-to-one clients, and the next doing a presentation or a motivational talk.

Success definitely isn't just about the medals and certificates. I'm very proud of what I achieved and being an elite athlete was amazing. But on a personal level, my wedding was the happiest day of my life.

A big part of success for me is being around my family, being relaxed and chilled; that's when life is good. All my medals are in a drawer at home; I don't have them on display any more because my focus is on the present and the future. I enjoy the swimming, but in a different way to how I did when I was competing all over the world. Now I get a kick out of coaching the next winners, and I enjoy open-water swimming in the endurance races I do.

It doesn't matter if I'm thinking about winning medals or reaching a new fitness target, my attitude when I've achieved what I set out to do is simple: 'I've done it, nice one.' Then I just think of the next thing, the next goal, and the next challenge. When I win a race, there's no ego, it's more like, 'What am I going to do now?'

Am I successful? Yes. But there's always something else I want to achieve. Success comes in two parts: what you've done and what comes next. I'm just not very good at sitting still.

Dan Pepper is a former Paralympic athlete and multi-award-winning elite swimmer. He won gold in both European and world championships events organised by the International Paralympic Committee once athletes with intellectual disabilities were reinstated into the Paralympic programme in 2012. In 2015 he was appointed as a high-performance athlete ambassador for the national campaign 'My Sport, My Voice!', run by the UK Sports

Association for People with Learning Disability. The campaign highlights the achievements of learning-disabled athletes and inspires others to succeed. Dan is also head coach at Marple Swimming Club in Stockport, the club where he first learned to swim aged four. He runs his own personal training business and regularly takes part in outdoor endurance events around the UK.

Laura's World

Laura Broughton

I create art because that's what I can do without having to think too hard.

I was born with hydrocephalus, which is a build-up of fluid on the brain, and it means I have a learning disability. I sometimes find things confusing. I struggle to keep up with conversations or follow directions. Things have to be explained to me many, many times before I understand. I know what I want to say – I have the words – but they can often feel a bit jumbled in my mind. Most people have an autopilot function in their daily interactions with each other, but this just isn't there for me.

The process of reading is also a challenge. I have to focus on one word at a time, so by the time I get to the end of a sentence, I've forgotten what the first words are. I need help with writing things down. Writing this essay would be impossible if I didn't have someone sitting with me, helping me write down my thoughts, helping me order them. In an ideal world, I'd rather sit and doodle than work on this bit of writing. But I know it's important to tell my story.

I have difficulties – but I lose them in the moment of creating. When I draw, I go from finding life difficult to finding that life becomes clearer. I don't need to work out a social situation or try to understand what people are saying. That all has to stop. I can focus on art and nothing else matters, so that's why I enjoy it. When I draw or paint, all I have to think about is what I'm creating. I call it being in 'Laura's world'. Making artwork gives me the opportunity to focus on one thing. I don't have to think about who said what, or what I'm doing in the next hour. It's about the fact that I don't have to talk.

I wouldn't call myself a painter – to me that means acrylics and oils and all that posh stuff. Although I do use acrylics and oils sometimes, I feel more at home using watercolour ink and pens. So what I do is a cross between drawing and painting. I don't like to be put into a box and I see myself as a person with a disability rather than a learning disability. That's because as well as a learning disability, I have epilepsy and weakness in my right side.

At weekends, I often take myself off into central London and sit on the edge of the pavement with my sketchbook, a coffee and my iPod. My sketchbook goes everywhere with me; it's like a diary. I listen to music and I start drawing. I plug in my headphones and it's a welcome disconnect from everything rushing around me. I was in Oxford Street, sitting at a bus stop with my sketchbook, when this guy came up and asked if he could take a photograph of me. I suppose he thought I was a 'street artist'. Once, I was drawing while sitting on the pavement in Covent Garden and some tourists tried to give me money. Maybe they thought I was homeless. I've had so many experiences through my art.

I like people-watching in busy places, where I see everyone rushing around. Society seems to say that you've got to go at this speed or you don't go anywhere, and I don't understand that. I like to sit quietly somewhere and watch it all happening. I often paint people in the city because the pace and vibrancy of city life both excites and terrifies me. I'm interested in finding my way through the crowds at rush hour, the towering backdrop of overbearing buildings, traffic, and people of all shapes, colours and sizes.

Through my art studies, I've had to explain how I work and I've had help in describing this from my art tutors and my family. I have support to write my artist's statements, and in these I often describe what I do as exploring the movements of people in their environment. I look to capture their character through line and colour. As we put one foot in front of the other, our bodies make different shapes. The space our bodies occupy and the spaces in between are constantly changing. These relationships interest me. I translate these scenes to create a sense of quietness. A break from it all, freeze-framing a moment of time.

My art is another way to see into my world.

Laura Broughton
Extracts from artist's statements

'Seeing' is hard to define. There is so much more to most things than meets the eye. Each of us sees things differently each time we look. I've been interested in looking at the space I take up, the way others respond to me and the way other people use their space. Expressing how I see myself and others, how I feel and navigate the madness of city life are concerns that have occupied my thoughts and my painting.

While elbowing my way through the broken, mixed-up, high-speed city life to find space and identity, I have discovered that neatness matters, a sense of place matters, control and order matters. I have uncovered lies, limitations and stupidity, as well as the colourful beauty of human life.

I am often unable to express much of the stuff in my mind, thinking of one thing and – before being able to see it through – going on to another. I find myself aspiring to something but not able to get there, and imagining what it would be like if I could.

I want a place and a voice. The making of a painting seems to somehow give me sense of 'having a voice' in a world of 'freedom of speech'.

Finding my way through my own human limitations has caused me to want to paint. To deliberately give place to my shape, skin, cloth, metal, wall, coat, car, etc. – the relationship between my body and the world around me.

Feelings of loss and struggle continue to interest me. I encounter characterless people going places, often in a great hurry, en route to somewhere but passing by. Unseeing, see-through, seemingly 'empty' people. I notice, I am not noticed. Thoughts often run into one another, not making sense in much the same way as people passing in the street.

I paint this emptiness, this 'un-seeingness', and by creating a semi-real fantasy world I aim to provide a momentary pause, a non-place, for reflection and recognition.

My mum, Esther, is the reason I do art. I wouldn't have got this far if it hadn't been for Mum's input. She knew I had it in me; she saw something and wanted to enable and encourage it. She's done it for each of her children because my three brothers are also creative in different ways (one designs shoes, one's a tree surgeon and the third works in public relations). My parents divorced when I was young, so as a single parent, my mum put all her energy into us kids.

My mum gave me the freedom to explore my abilities as an artist; she was a bit like a mentor. When I was at primary school in Norfolk, I had a tough time because I felt I didn't fit in. I don't remember much about it, but Mum says she suggested I should try drawing how I felt, and it started from there. I remember feeling a bit rubbish one day, so I drew a stick dog with some dog poop next to it. It started with that sort of thing, drawing as an outlet. I remember Mum saying that if I couldn't communicate how I felt by speaking, then I could try and draw it instead. I guess it was her who taught me to draw through feeling, rather than just through looking.

Painting gives me a sense of 'having a voice' because I can express myself through colour and texture.

When I was about eleven and my doodles were getting more like sketches of people or places, Mum suggested I do a page of drawing every day to improve my skills and confidence with using pencils. I went through a stage of loving to draw elephants. My mum had photographs from when she travelled to Africa, and these inspired me. Elephants also reflected the fact I felt clumsy, like I wasn't really moving like a human. Everything felt like it was three times harder than it was for everyone else. It was like I was trying to do these things like catch a ball or run, but it wasn't working because my hand wasn't flipping well working, or I was tripping up.

Mum said, 'If you want to draw elephants, you have to understand them and how they work.' So we'd get books and I'd study how they looked and moved. I suppose drawing's like doing an essay when you have to start from the basics and build up the argument.

My mum is artistic too, but she was so busy helping me to get to where I am today, she hasn't had time to do anything with her own art. She went to Camberwell College of Arts in London when she was younger, one of the best places to do art in the country. She probably could have gone on to the Slade School of Fine Art in London too, which is even better known. She could have made a living out of art and design. But she took the role of being a mother and supporting my education rather than her own. I know she's proud of me.

My first memory of school was of struggling and getting bullied. I went to the local secondary, but I had some of my lessons in what was called the 'special needs room', extra English and that sort of thing.

From what I can remember, I looked a little less able than I do now. My right arm was bent, and I wore orthopaedic boots that had buckles and metal hooks. I wore round NHS glasses that had long arms that curved round behind my ears so they'd stay on. I was therefore very different from everyone else at the school. The fact is that if you fell over, you either got laughed at or ignored, not shown compassion. Because I fell over a lot, I tended to get laughed at.

Mum knew I was unhappy so she moved me to a Montessori school. She explained to me that it was much more about learning through play and being creative. The headteacher was arty (the artist Ben Nicholson was her great-grandfather) and it felt like I was finding out about the world through looking at maps and talking, rather than looking at academic books. One thing I did enjoy at school was riding horses. Instead of some lessons, like PE or geography, I'd escape for a session at a local Riding for the Disabled centre.

I didn't do well at school, although I did get one GCSE, in art. But I needed GCSE English to do an art foundation course. By now I knew I wanted to carry on studying art, so I redid GCSE English at a local college and got on to an art foundation course at the City & Guilds of London Art School after we moved down to London from Norfolk.

At my end-of-year show for my foundation course, the pieces I showed were to do with my interest in the brain and the body. The pieces included paintings of elephants, brain scans, a porter chair (the type of hospital wheelchair which you can't push yourself but has to be pushed by someone else) and a depiction of me as a child with a ball in my hand.

The elephants were to do with movement and a link to what I used to draw with Mum. The brain scan was to do with the investigations doctors did for my hydrocephalus and the porter chair reminded me of my hospital treatment. The image of me as a child with a ball was because I was told by the doctors that if I squeezed a ball then the weakness in my hand would improve.

It felt exciting seeing my end-of-year show. It stood for the fact that actually I could do something, rather than me just seeing life as this big challenge. The bigger achievement after the foundation course was getting on to a degree course. I'd always wanted to go to university, but I never expected to be able to. Getting the foundation course under my belt meant I could apply for the BA in Fine Art at City & Guilds London Art School.

The art school itself describes the course as 'one of the most challenging and creative courses you can study', so as well as being over the moon at being accepted, I was slightly freaked out. I was overwhelmed, shocked that it was possible. You dream of something that you hope might be possible, but you're not quite sure because your disabilities might get in the way. You don't really know if it's possible to dream. It was like I didn't allow myself to get excited in case the thing I wanted didn't quite happen.

I didn't have the confident personality I have now – I was a shy girl then. At the start of my degree, to put it bluntly, I was shitting myself. The reading lists were crazy and I struggled with that. For some of my written work I submitted tape recordings, and fortunately I had Mum to help interpret my thoughts and help with the writing. There was no one else like me there on that course, which I was proud of because I'd got there on the merit of my art. The way Mum described it to me at the time, the tutors saw me and my skill; they didn't see me as someone with a disability.

Around this time I began drawing hands a lot. That was to do with wanting to understand myself. I wanted to look at my disability through my hands, using them to draw and as a subject. My other work during my degree included paintings of New York taxis. I had the idea that someone could look at these paintings and take themselves somewhere else – and it had nothing to do with disability.

I was inspired by a trip to New York that I won a college bursary to go on. I went on this amazing two-week trip, supported by a family friend. We went to loads of the museums and galleries, and it was incredible to see the famous buildings and the yellow cabs that I'd seen on television. I'd never gone beyond Europe before, not without my mum. Going to New York was a pretty big deal.

London and New York particularly inspire me because of the similarities and contrasts. Black cabs and yellow taxis, language, rich and poor; both cultures seem to be obsessed with the celebrity lifestyle too. I was painting things to do with the city that were constantly on my mind. What my art tutors told me was that it was as if I was reliving and experiencing something new with each painting.

*

I wouldn't be where I am today without my mum, Esther, so I asked her to write a few words about me from her point of view:

Laura's use of shape and colour has always been unusual. She seems to see things differently and this brings the characteristics of her subject to the fore.

Personally, I've always been visually aware – I love travel, art and architecture. I'm also inspired by nature: space, water, light and colour, whether that's to do with what to wear, things around me in the house or outside. Laura's grown up with me noticing and enthusiastically pointing out things like this.

Laura's Montessori head teacher took her on field trips from the age of nine, and got the kids to look at the world around them through a prism. Prisms split light into a rainbow of colour, giving a beautiful view of the world. Laura loved it.

If someone's creativity is stifled, it turns inward, causing depression and anxiety. So it's vital for Laura to express herself. But in a world favouring literacy, social media and celebrity, it can be hard for someone like Laura to find a voice.

Laura sustained brain damage from birth and has had many medical interventions over the years. She has to deal with epileptic seizures, learning and mobility difficulties, and relational and communication challenges. These are often hidden, and people generally have too much going on to take the time needed to understand and connect with Laura.

Through drawing, Laura's found an outlet for her soul, a way to make sense of and connect her inner and outer worlds and tell her story.

For Laura, dealing with life is like navigating and negotiating in a foreign language. She often needs me to understand events and interactions and re-present or explain them to her in different ways until she 'gets it'. The nuances within relationships, the nuances of language and the written word often trip her up.

Growing up, Laura used to literally trip up several times every day. She would often hurt herself but eventually she mastered walking and now just needs to watch the floor surface and be aware of her surroundings to be safe, but she does still occasionally fall. Everything Laura achieves is because it has been learned longhand – by repeating and repeating and repeating many, many, many times over and over again. It can be a frightening world.

I help Laura to understand what she's dealing with. I tease out the strands and look at them with her. We talk about things that are bothering her. Once unravelled, she can then decide what she wants to do and I can help her to go to the right place or person.

So, for example, a text will come in saying several things at once to do with making arrangements to meet. There may be lots of date options and ideas. This overwhelms Laura and she will often tell me what it says and ask how to answer. It's a bit like a kid with a shape sorter – relationships and conversations need deciphering. With me helping her with this, it frees her up to get on with her work.

I am *very* proud of Laura. She's courageous and clever. She's an inspiration for anyone who truly meets her – and by that I mean anyone who takes time to properly connect with her. Laura describes herself with candour and without self-pity, and she retains a beautiful guilelessness that most of us have lost along the way.

I would love more people to encounter Laura's kindness and humour while better understanding her limitations – and her strengths.

In the fine-art world, there's a lot of academic thinking and it's hard for me to keep up with that. You have to have an awareness of the 'journey' between starting a piece of artwork and finishing it. It's about the process, or the conversation you have about it, not just the actual artwork in front of you. It's about contextualising your work, concepts and interpretation, rather than thinking, *I'm doing this piece of artwork because I want to do it.* The thing is, my natural approach is just to create the piece of work, to feel it and do it. I don't like to overthink it or worry about the academic process of how I've got there.

I also don't necessarily want to tell people what they should see in something I've made. I create it for other people to interpret rather than for me to communicate a particular thought. I can draw, but I don't always draw realistically. What I do is more of an impressionistic interpretation. I don't fit into a mould myself, and you can say that about my artwork as well.

I once did a series of dreamlike, abstract pieces exploring

the sensations just before having an epileptic fit. These explored the idea of what it's like when something is just about to happen.

When I'm drawing or painting people, I often use eyes as a way to indicate the idea that people are always looking at you, observing you. Social interaction interests me because sometimes I find it so hard. I think people's characteristics are often displayed through their eyes or hands. I draw to get across something of the often quirky nature of how I see, and to provoke a smile.

My work is influenced by what I see and experience, but I've also been inspired by other artists who I've found out about through my art studies. I've looked at Jean-Michel Basquiat and Grayson Perry for the playful quality of lines and colour, the overlapping images and use of words. I also like the work of Philip Guston for its humour, colour and cartoon-like style, and the expressive eyes in Lee Bontecou's work.

I like the colour contrasts in Craigie Aitchison's pieces and how Frida Kahlo communicates her pain. But it's not like I'll automatically look at a work of art and think, *Oh yes, I know what Frida Kahlo's trying to 'say' in this piece.* I don't automatically look at a piece of art and analyse it. It's taken me a really long time, through studying art and talking through my thoughts with Mum or my art tutors, to understand that. Other sources for my work include anatomy books for the structure of the body and images from magazines of fast-moving cars and scenery.

I've exhibited in various London galleries and venues, like the Cadogan Contemporary and the City Lit college, but my standout moment was being accepted for the Royal Academy Summer Exhibition.

The Royal Academy's what I call a 'bee's knees' name, and it was a massive goal of mine to be in it. To be one of over a thousand artists whose pieces were chosen from 12,000 submissions – that was my proudest moment.

The piece that was selected was a pencil on paper line drawing called *Post Party*. It showed a figure curled up on a chair, reading. My tutor at the Royal Drawing School sat for me and the piece took me half a day to do. It was sold to a private buyer almost immediately when the show opened. Having my submission chosen for the UK's biggest open art exhibition made me feel equal because I was judged against the same standard as all the other artists without disabilities.

If you look like you've got a disability, society treats you a little bit like a child, which I can't stand. But if people treat you or talk to you like an average Joe Bloggs, you can sometimes get confused. When someone talks really fast, I don't always hear every word in the sentence, so I jump from one sentence to another to get away from the fact that it's a problem, and I miss stuff. I don't want to be treated like a child just because I'm disabled, but at the same time, I might need you to speak more plainly or less fast.

Things can be difficult because I don't 'look' disabled. Like Mum says, I have an invisible disability, which can make life really hard. One scenario was when I was on a bus and a bus inspector asked to see everyone's passes. He looked at my Freedom pass, which gives me free travel on public transport because I've got a disability, and said, 'You don't look like you've got disabilities.' I said, 'Well, I do have a disability.' I wasn't really shocked when he said that, but I didn't like being singled out and questioned.

It's like when I went out for a drink with a few people from my drawing classes, and someone asked why I wasn't drinking more beer. I didn't really want to talk about my epilepsy but in the end I had to explain that too much alcohol could trigger a seizure. Can't I have just the one drink without someone asking why I'm not drinking more? So I ended up having to say I'm epileptic and that, of course, then raises more questions and I get anxious. So that's the sort of thing I struggle with.

When these things happen, these situations that are frustrating, this is what feels like 'Laura's world'. Say if you meet me and I say, 'Hi, I'm Laura, I create paintings and do arty things and I work in social care,' then you can cope because there are two boxes you can put me in. But as soon as you start asking, 'Why don't you work full time?' or, 'Why don't you drive?' then it all becomes a big can of worms. You'll want to know my whole history, and I don't really want to have to go into the fact I was premature at birth, and that's where the problems come from. I find it annoying and frustrating and it makes me anxious.

The older you get though, the more you get used to these things. 'Laura's world' is about the interpretations and interactions. It's about how people interact with me – or don't.

*

My career in social care started at the beginning of 2011 through the care provider that supports me, Choice Support. I rent my own place in London, but I get help from Choice Support with things that I can find difficult.

My support worker helps me manage my finances and make appointments. I also get support with keeping up with household chores, cleaning, cooking, shopping, writing emails, working out my social calendar and anything to do with my art commitments, like organising exhibitions.

How I got into social care was that I had a care review meeting a few years ago (this is where your support staff go over what you want to get out of your support, or what you might need more or less help with). I said I had a goal to become more assertive because I often hesitated to ask people to repeat what they'd said if I didn't quite hear them, and that this was holding me back. With Choice Support's help, I designed a training package about speaking up that I could deliver to other social care organisations. We spent several weeks preparing the training material, and I practised so I could present it professionally.

The first session was a success, the feedback was positive and the bookings for more sessions came flying in. My confidence grew and I became more self-assured about my new role.

After this I became an 'Expert by Experience' for five years. The Experts by Experience project is an initiative from the Care Quality Commission, the organisation that regulates health and social care. It means that people with user or carer experience get involved in inspecting the kind of services they might use or have used in the past. It can be anything from a residential care home to a long-stay hospital. Through doing the inspections and my speaking work, I got to be quite well known at training days or conferences to do with social care. I started to be sought out for talks across the country.

As part of my inspector role, I was involved in the inspections of 150 learning disability services that happened after the Winterbourne View scandal, to try and make sure that kind of thing didn't happen again. Winterbourne View was a hospital unit where people with learning disabilities were being abused by staff. People only found out about the awful things that went on there because the BBC did undercover filming there. Working on the inspections gave me the experience of what it's really like for other people who have a learning disability. What happened at Winterbourne View was terrible and should have never happened.

One of the things that came up a lot on the inspections was that staff did things for individuals, rather than them being able to do things for themselves. In one care home, I spotted that the stairs only had handrails on one side. The weakness in my right side means I need rails on both sides, so I told the home about this. Some people had drinks only at mealtimes, but they needed to be offered drinks regularly, because they couldn't verbally ask for one and weren't able to get up and get one when they wanted one.

Some of the people I met should have had more help in getting a better life. They were often bored and distressed, and staff talked to them not as adults but as though they were children. Some of the people weren't treated as individuals. I felt some people didn't get the opportunities they should have because they couldn't speak or because others felt their behaviour was challenging. I can identify with that. It struck me that in a sense I was very like that person who I'd meet on inspections. It's just that I've had the right influence to enable me to be who I am.

A few years ago I was speaking at an event run by Paradigm, a training and development agency that works with organisations specialising in learning disability care. The managing director was so impressed with my experience and contribution that she asked me if I'd be interested in helping deliver some more training. My work with Paradigm went so well that eventually I was asked to join the organisation as an associate consultant. I've done things like public speaking, standing up in a room full of 200 people, which has grown my skills and made me more assertive.

Last year, the art and the social care worlds I work in came together when I was appointed as an artist-in-residence at London South Bank University. It's a brilliant opportunity to showcase my work. However, it's been frustrating because I've struggled with getting hold of information (like how to get onto the campus and how to get hold of an entry pass). It's just another reminder that nothing is ever plain sailing.

The funny thing is, years ago I did a health and social care course after I left school. I only really did it because a family friend had done the same course. It was also something to get a qualification in and the college was close to where I lived. I did it for convenience, but years later I've ended up working in social care.

My social care work pays me, it supports my independence and develops my confidence. When I started all this, it was quite nerve-racking but exciting at the same time. It's a good experience in terms of people appreciating me and my knowledge. Not like in the past, when people could only see me as a disabled person. It also makes me feel a little bit more like I'm part of something, valued as a person in my own right. Having a paid job is new for me, as it is with a lot of people who have a learning disability. I have a voice, and through my work inspecting care homes, I've been able to help other people living in these services to have a voice too.

What I love about the social care work is having the opportunity to see different places and to do different things. But if I didn't have the support then I couldn't and wouldn't have my career in social care. It's me doing this work, but to enable me to do it to the best of my abilities there has to be a system in place. The elements that Choice Support makes happen, like someone helping type up my notes, or giving a bit of help with invoices, means I can focus on the actual work, which I'm good at. It's not necessarily that I couldn't do my work without that help, but I would be scared, as I wouldn't know how to cope with the other bits like the administrative stuff that you have to have in place. If these systems weren't in place then I'd be having seizures because I wouldn't know how to deal with the official and financial side of it.

*

I've managed this much, which is quite extraordinary, and now I want to learn more. I want to learn about the history of art, so I can find out more about who or what I'm influenced with. Sometimes I can't remember who the artist is that I like, or what school or movement they're from. I want and need more knowledge to be able to take my art forward. Sometimes I think I'm not academically an artist because I haven't got to grips with who I am influenced by. An MA in Art at the Royal Academy would be a good thing to do and in the future I'd love to own my own studio. That would be amazing.

To make sure more people can do what I do, the people who teach art have to be more creative with their teaching. When you learn to walk, you have to do it step by step. If you're teaching a person that has difficulties, it doesn't necessarily have to be step-by-step forwards. It can be sideways, it can be backwards, it can go off course a bit, but eventually it will be a forward direction if the person you're teaching has enough determination.

It's like rather than saying, 'I'm teaching you to count to ten, so it's one, two, three, four, five,' you teach somebody 'one, four, six and eight' – if that feels more comfortable for them – and they'll eventually get the 'one, two, three, four, five'. You just have to think about it in a different way. The usual interpretation of the world and the way school teaches you is a load of crap if you're a person that doesn't understand the things or the systems that society says you have to. It's like me going to a Montessori school, where they didn't necessarily teach me through books but through play or creativity – they enable you to learn even if it is not the same way as everybody else. If I hadn't had help in making sense of the world from my mum and my support workers, I wouldn't have been successful.

I look back at myself twenty years ago and I couldn't ever have seen myself not living with my mum, or knowing what I was going to do for the rest of my life. I had the dream of living on my own, of having my independence, working and making art, but I didn't realise what was possible. And now I'm doing it. It's a way to achieve happiness for me. It's no different from anyone else really, even the difficult times, because everybody feels restricted in their way of life at some stage, or has problems. It's funny, because I don't see art as my career as such, because my art is my way of life. But anyway, that's me.

In 2016, Laura Broughton became the first woman with a learning disability to win a place at the Royal Academy of Arts Summer Exhibition. Her pencil drawing was one of 1,240 chosen from 12,000 submissions to the annual show. Laura is an artist-in-residence at South Bank University and has a BA in Fine Art Painting and a postgraduate diploma from the Royal Drawing School. Laura also has a career in social care as a consultant and trainer. Laura was involved in helping a nationwide programme of inspections of learning disability services following the Winterbourne View scandal in 2011, where staff in an NHS-funded residential hospital in South Gloucestershire had been abusing learning-disabled people.

Sparkle and Space

Matthew Hellett

I'm a filmmaker and a performer. I have a learning disability and I'm gay. My work gives me a voice and a chance to tell people who I am.

Mrs Sparkle is my drag queen alter ego. She's adventurous and a bullshitter. She's sassy and a law unto herself. Being Mrs Sparkle lets everybody know who I am. I co-wrote and featured in a short black-and-white film about my drag act in 2008. It was called *Sparkle* and it explains what the character of Mrs Sparkle means to me. The film premiered at the Curzon Cinema in Mayfair in London and won the best documentary award at the Picture This Film Festival in Calgary, Canada.

This is an edited extract from my script for *Sparkle*:

I want to get out of this life that isn't a dream. After all this time I think I deserve a bit of happiness for myself… because I've always been such a worrier, really. I would like to have a happy and fulfilling life – a nice sense of happiness all around me, buzzing everywhere. Because we are all put here for some sort of reason. All the silly little trivial anxieties that I have – sometimes a big struggle, really. And then I get my make-up. Oh yes, she comes from my heart, like an imaginary friend. It feels like I'm acting, like a famous person, and I don't have to worry about anything any more. It just feels like there are no more frustrations or anxieties because they've all gone. It feels fabulous, yeah. Well, I look and feel fantastic. And I'm Mrs Sparkle. And it's just brilliant. It's almost like she lives in another world because she gives herself an inner peace, an inner happiness. And I can sleep knowing that I've made people smile and giggle, and it's always a privilege, really.

I devised the character of Mrs Sparkle when I was invited to be a host at the Blue Camel, a club night in Brighton for people with learning disabilities. I didn't have this alter ego until then, and I thought I'd give dressing up a go as an experiment, and it just went from there.

For my very first appearance as Mrs Sparkle, I had on silver platforms and a red catsuit and I wore gold eyeliner. I was really nervous. The shoes were a bit deadly – I almost tripped coming on stage. I remember thinking, *It's all going to go Pete Tong*. But in fact it went quite well, better than I expected. I did some lip-syncing to 'Shout' by Lulu. I really enjoyed performing and I could tell the audience felt quite excited. I loved the fact they liked what I did and I made people smile and laugh. I always want the audience to have some fun and excitement and humour. I want them to feel enthusiastic, like they're getting something from my performance as Mrs Sparkle. And there's definitely a bit of me in her.

Mrs Sparkle's routine usually involves a bit of a walkabout and banter. She just goes up to people and talks. I've written some shocking storylines for Mrs Sparkle over the years, like when her babies were going to be taken away by social services because she was a bad mother. Once, she turned up in an orange jumpsuit because she'd got herself arrested and been in prison. She's a terrible mother, really awful; she's always on the piss.

I don't think I'd have developed the character of Mrs Sparkle if I wasn't living in Brighton and wasn't involved with Carousel. Carousel is the learning disability arts charity that runs the Blue Camel Club. I came across Carousel in my twenties and I love the fact that its aim is to show how learning-disabled artists can make really great art. The idea is that people are put in control of their own films, music or performances – it's done by us, not *for* us. All the work is planned, managed and delivered by us, and several board members have a learning disability.

I've been involved in so many of Carousel's projects over the last twenty years. I've co-tutored a dance course for young people with a learning disability. I performed in *Debbie Rock Angel*, which was the world's first rock opera created by learning-disabled musicians, performers and filmmakers. The show was supported by Carousel, the Glyndebourne opera house and South East Dance. I've scripted, directed and featured in a short film, *Unusual*

Journey, which promoted sustainable transport in Brighton. Fatboy Slim screened the film at a New Year's Day gig on Brighton Beach. I was also the first learning-disabled filmmaker to win a commission from South East Dance for another film, *Mrs Sparkle*, which premiered at Carousel's film festival, Oska Bright, in 2009.

Oska Bright started in 2004. It happens every two years in Brighton and runs for three days. The name is a play on the name Oscar – like the Hollywood Oscars – and Bright is for Brighton, where the festival's held. I'm the programme manager, so I help run the event along with a team of learning-disabled artists. We showcase films made by people with a learning disability from around the world. It's very much our own festival, but if we need a hand with anything, there are staff at Carousel who don't have learning disabilities who can help if we need it.

At our last festival, we screened over sixty films that were either made by learning-disabled people or included learning-disabled people. We had 3,500 people come to the last festival and we've had over 5,000 films submitted since the festival began. We also take the event on tour and over the last few years I've been everywhere from London to Newcastle and Canada, Australia and Prague. A few years ago, we took the festival to the Adelaide International Film Festival in Australia, and it inspired the launch of another disability-led festival, Sit Down, Shut Up and Watch. That's something I'm really proud of.

When people have more control over their art, they 'own' it, because they tell their own stories in their own way. The work they produce is, I think, more real. Also, if you do something yourself and it doesn't go how you planned it, you can learn from that and make it better. For example, when the film festival started, some of the films weren't very good. That's because they were the first of their kind. But we did a filmmaking guide and put it on the Carousel website so people could develop their skills. Also, we take the festival on the road and we run masterclasses and workshops, so people pick up tips on how to make films. Now the films entered into the festival are of a much higher quality.

As the festival's programme manager it's my job to decide what gets shown, and I also organise the films that are submitted into themes. I'm honoured to watch all these amazing films. I pick out the subjects and tie everything together.

It was my idea to include a new LGBT strand for the first time in 2017. That was a huge achievement for me. I called it Queer Freedom, because it celebrates the queer community, love and self-expression. The strand came about because at a previous festival I'd met an incredible artist called Matthew Kennedy. Matthew's a queer/femme filmmaker and we hit it off straight away. He's the first learning-disabled LGBT filmmaker I've met, so he really understands what it's like to be me. Meeting Matthew made me realise that we need to give the space to more unheard voices. I'm a gay learning-disabled man, and I love to do drag. I don't have that many friends in the gay community and it's important for us to come together, support each other and celebrate the work we do as artists.

In the new queer strand, I wanted to get across the idea that we treat everybody the same and that everybody's welcome. My idea was to champion the voice of every person with learning disabilities. I didn't want to leave anyone out. The festival is totally committed to pushing the representation of all learning-disabled people, gay or straight. Also, it's important to me that it isn't just a film festival for learning-disabled people. We believe that the stories and films we show are ones that people everywhere should see – because they're amazing films. At our last festival, 54 per cent of our audience didn't have a learning disability.

Before we showed the queer strand, I thought, *Is it going to work or will it be too controversial?* But I decided to just do it, go for it – and it worked really well; in fact, it went down a storm. The films included this really beautiful short animation, *John and Michael*, which was a love story between two men with Down's syndrome. There was another short, *Life on Two Spectrums*, about Tia Anna finding her way as a drag queen and developing her character's routine. As a drag artist myself, I really identified with the film.

I don't find it hard choosing which films to include in the programme. I know in the first five minutes whether something will work or not, if it looks amazing or if it's trash. It's got to grab people and it's about quality, not quantity. We also screen young people's films because we want to support the next generation of filmmakers. I want to keep inspiring young people to keep making work and develop their skills. I spend a lot of my time looking for new talent and encouraging more people to get involved with Oska Bright. We've got our regular filmmakers, but we also get younger people coming through all the time, so we mustn't ignore them. I think my work's groundbreaking, so I hope it makes it easier for younger people to do what I'm doing. If I can do it, they can too.

I enjoy everything about making a film. If I wasn't able to be creative, it would feel like there was something really big missing from my life. Making films gives me a creative energy, a buzz. Without it my life would be a horrible dark cloud that hasn't got any blue sky in it.

I get something different from performing, something that's quite theatrical. On a performing day, compared to a filmmaking day, it's like I'm not actually Matthew because I take on this new persona. I could be someone else completely. I love that. I also like making films because you get more creative input into the whole process; you drive it from start to finish. In my head, it's like being the captain of a cruise ship, steering it through the sea.

I grew up in Brighton. Looking back, school wasn't great. I went to a Catholic comprehensive where the staff were nice enough, but it was pretty rubbish for people with learning disabilities.

There wasn't really much extra help with things like English or maths, so I used to go to the art room at break time. That was my escape. I had a fantastic art teacher, Mrs Elliot, and her room was my comfortable outlet. I just wanted to express myself and the art room was the only way. She'd just let me draw. She was one of my favourite teachers; I guess she was a bit like a mentor. She asked what my favourite book was and I told her it was Enid Blyton's Famous Five stories (I was one of five children). So she asked me to produce a painting based on that. I still have it framed on my wall. Mrs Elliot encouraged me to be creative.

I left school at sixteen without doing any exams, and I went to a further-education college for people with learning disabilities. This was a place where they did practical stuff, like cooking. They didn't really do things like the arts. It was really sad because I would have loved to do some acting at school or college, just something artistic to help me thrive. But I wasn't given the opportunity, even when I said, 'This is what I want to do.' They said, 'We don't have the facilities.' It was really frustrating.

It was through my family that I got my love of film. We had some great trips to the cinema together. I remember this amazing trip to London when I was about ten and we went to see *The Sound of Music*. That was one of my favourite moments, all squeezed into this tiny little auditorium, seeing a film on the big screen. I liked it because it expresses freedom and it's got a happy ending. There were little children restricted by their dad until the nanny comes along, played by Julie Andrews, and she teaches them to sing. She gives them this creative opportunity.

We used to watch the Superman films at home too, and my dad and I would be in hysterics. We'd laugh about the fact this bloke in a suit goes into a phone box to get changed into this funny costume with his pants on over his tights. Something about it was amusing and silly. I don't think it was meant to be funny, but it made me laugh.

As a kid, watching films that made me laugh must have had an influence on what I do now, because comedy is such a big part of my drag routine and my filmmaking. My comedy hero would be Patsy from *Absolutely Fabulous*. I'm a bit like her, like I've got a filthy sense of humour. My friends say Patsy runs through my blood.

I also like Steven Spielberg's *E.T. the Extra-Terrestrial* – it made me cry when I saw it as a child. I love the bit when E.T. reaches out with his finger to make a connection with the little boy, Elliott.

I like feel-good films too, things like *Moulin Rouge*. I like films that aren't too sad and are led by the storyline. One thing I'm definitely not into is science fiction. Science fiction bores the pants off me and it's not my favourite genre, but we're all made differently, and I appreciate people that have different tastes from mine.

By the time I was twenty-one, before I'd come out or got started working with Carousel, I was living in a group home in Brighton for people with learning disabilities. I don't think moving out of my parents' place helped me become much more independent, although it should have done. I was still so young, and at the group home we only had a visit from a support worker once a day. That whole period of my life was so dull. I also had a part-time job working at a high-street store. My job was to sit at the computer all day and check what stock was being taken down to the shop floor. I got made redundant and moved to another group home in Epsom, Surrey. I didn't want to leave Brighton, but the care organisation that was supporting me at the time said that they had a house there with better facilities than the one in Brighton.

So I had to move fifty miles away to a crap town that I didn't know anything about and where I didn't know anyone. There wasn't a lot going on in Epsom, frankly. It was a boring, horrible house and I had this little room with a shower, so I had some privacy, but I shared the kitchen and lounge with this other guy. He had a learning disability too but we didn't have any similar interests.

The care organisation found me a job; they said it was 'therapeutic work'. There I was, sitting in an office mail room, stuffing letters into envelopes every day. It really wasn't me; I felt like the lowest of the low. If I'd been making art at that time, it would have done me the power of good. What was wrong with these people who were meant to be supporting me? They should have asked me, 'What are your hobbies and interests?' Not one person asked what would inspire me, what would make me happy. No one was interested in what I wanted to do with my life. I would have loved to have done some visual art, just something creative to express myself. And I was still so young, so I didn't feel I could refuse to do the work, or say what I really wanted to do.

I really wasn't happy there, so I eventually came back to Brighton after a couple of years and moved into a flat of my own, which was run by a different organisation, Southdown Housing. Southdown runs specialist housing where you get help from a care worker but you live more independently than in a group home. I couldn't believe it when staff there actually asked what my likes and dislikes were. They asked how I'd like to be supported and it made me feel a sense of belonging. It made me think they were actually interested in me and were listening to me.

It was during a chat with my support worker that I mentioned I wanted to do something creative, so I decided to make a film. That was my first film, a spoof cooking show called *Cooking With Matthew*, which I made in 2006. The film grew from my wicked sense of humour and led me to get involved with Carousel. My support worker helped me put it together and it just seemed to flow really easily and I improvised a lot of it. The film shows me cooking and it's surreal and quirky. So you see me frying a piece of salmon, but instead of using cream in the sauce, I use a big pot of white paint. There's a silly bit when I get an idea for what to use in the recipe and a light bulb pops up on screen over my head. It's just a bit different and it's based on what I find amusing.

The whole thing took about three months to make. First I storyboarded the film and worked out what props I needed and what shots might work. Then I scripted it, and my support worker helped me set up the shots and filmed the bits I was in. He also encouraged me to put the film in to a local film festival, Oska Bright, which I'd never heard of. It ended up winning an award for best overall film that year.

The fact that the first film I'd made won an award was incredible. I felt really excited about going to the festival. It was like suddenly there was a chance to do this new thing. It felt amazing, a platform to show my first piece of work. If that support worker hadn't known about this, it might not have happened. When I went up to collect the gong, it felt really good holding it. It made me think, *I'm going to do more of this*. Winning inspired me to carry on being creative and, not long after, Carousel asked me to join the festival team and that's when the ball got rolling.

I remember that first time I walked through the door at Carousel, almost twenty years ago. I was young and immature and didn't know which creative direction I wanted to take; I didn't know exactly what I wanted to do to express myself. It was scary and unknown. But I knew I wanted to be creative, and Carousel helped me try all sorts of different things, from dance to singing and film. I also won a training bursary from the charity so I could learn how to develop my performance skills. I slowly got more insight into what I wanted to do, what I wanted to achieve and what I wanted to get out of being creative. I became more confident, almost like I got to know myself better.

When I think back to those days, it's like I was a little caterpillar before I started on this creative journey, and now I'm like a butterfly.

I didn't always know I was gay; I think I realised in my late teens. I had two straight relationships in my early twenties, but deep down I knew that wasn't me. I couldn't live a lie any longer because it was making me feel down. I didn't come out till I was twenty-seven because I grew up in a Catholic family and it wasn't easy coming out earlier.

I came out in Malta on holiday with my sister, Anne, who I'm really close to. We were on this beautiful beach with no one and nothing around except the sea and the birds. I felt I had enough headspace to finally come out. Anne wasn't surprised; she said she'd known for a long time I was gay. She said, 'I think it'll be all right because Mum and Dad love you. It might take a bit of time, but it will be all right.'

I told both my parents when I was visiting them, and I was so nervous. My late dad was just standing at the kitchen sink, and he didn't even stop washing up when I started talking. I think that was his way of not making a fuss and just accepting what I was telling him. My mum said, 'I thought you might be gay, but I wasn't sure, and we still love you.' My dad didn't say much, but he just carried on treating me as he always did.

Coming out was actually less difficult than I thought it might be. I just wish I'd come out a bit earlier, because when I did, I felt quite liberated and I just had this huge sense of relief. I knew I could be who I wanted to be if I came out. I didn't feel true to myself until then. Not long after I came out, I went to a gay nightclub, Heaven, in London. I had a great night with the energy of the music and dancing and getting sweatier by the moment. I felt I could just be myself. I didn't give a damn about how I was dancing or behaving, because everyone else was just being themselves in that environment.

Why can't we just allow people with learning disabilities to be sexual? I was so shocked when I watched the film *Sanctuary* to see if we could include it as part of Oska Bright. It's about the fact that until 2017 in Ireland it used to be illegal to have sex with someone who had a learning disability. So people with learning disabilities couldn't have sexual relationships. I was so proud that, later in 2017, our film festival gave the movie its UK premiere. I love the film; it's just so funny and moving and powerful. It touches different parts of your emotions and it's such an enlightened film. It tells the story of a young couple who meet in a care home and fall in love. They sneak off to a hotel to spend time together during a day trip. But it's against the law – I mean, oh my God, how can two adults not be allowed to have sex? People should be allowed to express themselves how they want and to be together if they want to.

Generally, if you have a learning disability, people don't ask you what you like to do, what your interests are or what you want to get out of life. It's like you're not a real person – and that goes for our sexuality too.

One time I was speaking at a conference about my work at the film festival, and I was talking about a film we'd shown that mentioned someone in their underwear. I couldn't believe it when a couple of people from the audience said it sounded inappropriate to be screened for people with learning disabilities. It's outrageous. People are being too protective, like they don't want to open up that door to sexuality. There's just this sad stereotype that means people who have a learning disability get treated like children.

But I have a human right to be me – I just couldn't be me if I lived in a place where I felt I had to behave a certain way to fit in. People should be able to live comfortably and freely in their community and be who they want to be. They should be able to be with whoever they want to be with, even though other people might feel a bit awkward about that.

In 2015 the screen industry organisation Creative Skillset did an employment report of the total UK workforce in film. It showed that people like me aren't represented in film – in front of or behind the camera. It's crazy and it shouldn't be like that.

I've used the figures from the survey in so many talks I've done, and they're shocking. Only 0.3 per cent of the total film workforce are disabled. Only 0.2 per cent work in production, 0.1 per cent work in exhibition – and that includes me – and none work in distribution. This makes me feel insignificant. It's pretty awful. How are we supposed to get into the industry?

There are over 13 million disabled people in the UK – that's one in four. So why aren't there more opportunities for us? About 18 per cent of the working-age population is disabled. We contribute to the economy and we spend around £50 billion each year. I'm pretty sure lots of that is spent on arts and entertainment. So where are the openings in the arts sector for us? People see the disability and not the person. The film industry is like a private members' club: it's hard to get into and sometimes, like other industries, it's based on who you know.

Even if you do see people with learning disabilities in film or on television, you get some really awful stereotypes. Blind people always want to feel everyone's face. Do you need to make a non-disabled actor look disabled? Just give them a bad haircut! The disabled person in a film usually spends the entire movie whining about how they want to die. And of course everyone with autism is great at maths. People have a narrow perception. They make judgments about people.

We always see extremes of disability and we never see NORMAL disabled people. So how can we change things? Companies don't understand that if they make reasonable adjustments like printing information in plain English, things could be more inclusive. The film industry is missing out on unique talents by ignoring creative people with physical disabilities and learning disabilities.

This is why I go on tour with our film festival around the UK and the world. We want to screen films that encourage learning-disabled audiences to come to the cinema and show what they can do behind the camera too. We know we need to do more to make the cinema experience more accessible to a wider audience.

Things are slowly changing, though. One good thing was when the British Film Institute invited me to go to Belfast to do some training on inclusion. I spent a long time talking to arts venues about how to be more inclusive and how to programme more inclusive content.

I was once asked at a conference if I did arts projects 'for therapy'. That attitude makes me so angry. It's not therapy

– it's art. When I've toured with Oska Bright all around the country and overseas, I've heard people saying things like the films were good and that everyone must have got a lot out of making them. People think that if we 'do art', it's at a day centre and it's something to keep ourselves busy with or it's some sort of healing or wellbeing treatment. I think it's stereotyping again.

We really need people to take learning-disabled artists more seriously. I think the films I programme are of a high quality and I think more people should see them. I've talked about this a lot over the years with my colleagues at Oska Bright and we decided to get together with other artists and performers with learning disabilities to see what we could do about this.

So, through Carousel, I was involved in a project called Creative Minds. We got a national debate going about learning-disabled artists and performers. We wanted to change people's ideas and thoughts and the way they see us. When we began talking with other learning-disabled artists, performers and filmmakers, we found out that everyone had lots of different experiences of not being taken seriously as artists. We want people to see us as proper creatives who can perform and present works that are as professional and as entertaining as artists without disabilities. Between 2014 and 2017 we had five Creative Minds conferences around the country, in Brighton, Bristol, Ipswich, Birmingham and Manchester.

What do we need to change? We need to get away from the idea that lots of people seem to have, which is that people with learning disabilities can't create or lead their own art. But we are perfectly capable of making our own art in our own unique and interesting ways. We need to make sure that people don't patronise us or look down at us, because that's like patting us on the back as if we're children.

For example, if someone tells us what to do in a performance – 'Walk on stage, turn round, say hello and walk off' – then we're not being creative. But if we make our own entrance and find our own creative style to move across a stage, then we're being creative, we're being ourselves. We think we can tell the difference between these two, and we think audiences can too.

Most of our work doesn't get talked about or reported on because people are afraid of hurting our feelings. We haven't been allowed to 'fail' or sometimes even to 'have a go'. But I think that it's good for other people to tell you what they like or don't like about your artwork. It helps us to improve what we do and to think more about what we do and why we do it. Most artists like to cause a bit of controversy – it's the same for learning-disabled artists.

We want to change this. Maybe our work isn't seen as good quality because we're often given opportunities under venues' 'education' or 'outreach' programmes. We're not engaged as 'quality' or 'professional' artists. Lots of learning disability arts organisations are known for putting on very high-quality projects. But there are hardly any named, individual learning-disabled artists who have a reputation under their own names.

Arts venues also need to get more people with learning disabilities into the audience. They need to think about what they need. Some people may have challenging behaviour and may make sudden noises and movements, so staff need to be there if people need assistance getting to their seats. A venue should keep choices simple, so that people aren't overwhelmed, like simple ticket and refreshment options. Why not film a walkthrough of your venue and record an audio tour, to help people get used to what will happen when they arrive. Then they'll know what can they expect.

A lot of cinemas now have 'autism-friendly screenings' where lights are left on or the sound isn't as loud as usual. These are great, but they're often aimed at younger people. They're on too early and it's often kids' films that are programmed. You don't stop being autistic at fifteen. So why not try to programme to everyone's tastes? Some people think that we only like kids' films. This isn't true: we're not children and we like all kinds of films.

My advice to the cinema chains is they should spend time speaking to local day centres, group homes and care organisations. Find out when they do their activities and when's a good time to have a screening for them. Weekends are bad for people with learning disabilities who live in group homes, because they often don't have support then and are stuck inside. Programming films and events for them during the daytime at weekends would be best.

A couple of years ago, I was selected for Guiding Lights, the UK film industry mentoring scheme, along with my Oska Bright colleague Becky Bruzas. Becky, who has a learning disability, also works on the festival. Over 200 people applied and when Becky and I got on to the mentoring project, it was the first time anyone with a learning disability had ever been part of it. It was empowering for us and, hopefully, for other learning-disabled filmmakers. We showed the world and other people that this is possible.

Emma Smart mentored me for a year. Emma co-programmes the London Lesbian and Gay Film Festival, the biggest LGBT film festival in Europe. She helped me to be fearless and trust my creative instincts. I learned how to have more creative control and it made me more picky. Doing the mentoring made me more clear about what I need to look for in the quality of a film. Emma also helped me realise that I could play on other people's qualities and interests and share the workload.

So, for example, I have no idea about science-fiction films (and I can't stand them!), so if someone submits a science-fiction short to the festival, I can delegate that to someone else on my team and play to their strengths. I also learned more about pitching work – such as giving people more eye contact (I sometimes just look down at my hands when I speak if I'm nervous). I definitely developed my confidence and learned more about programming when I was being mentored. It made me think more about what else I wanted to do, and that led me to launch the queer strand at Oska Bright.

I sometimes forget how much I have achieved, not because I have a problem with memory, but because I've done so much! Success for me is being able to express myself. When I was thinking about what to include in this essay, I looked up the actual meaning of the word 'success'. It is 'the accomplishment of an aim or purpose'. So, my aim is to have the right space artistically to express myself. I was born with this need to express myself, but I didn't always have the space to achieve it. For me, Brighton is a creative city that allows me to be myself, and Carousel's given me a platform to show what I can do.

A lot of people with learning disabilities don't have that. That's not good at all. No one should be afraid of achieving their goals. I don't think anyone should let anything get in their way, because life is too short and too precious. We're all here for a purpose, for a reason, and everybody needs to have space to have their goals and achievements and to achieve something. People might not like my drag act or my films. They might not understand my learning disability or the fact I'm gay. But I reckon you either like it or you get lost, or at least that's my theory.

Matthew Hellett is an award-winning filmmaker, performer and drag artist from Brighton. He is the head programmer of the Oska Bright Film Festival in Brighton, a biennial festival and touring programme featuring short films and digital media that include people with a learning disability. In 2017, Matthew introduced a groundbreaking queer strand to the festival. He is one of the first two people with a learning disability to have been accepted on to the UK film industry mentoring programme Guiding Lights. As a leading member of the campaign group Creative Minds,

Matthew promotes quality in learning disability art and raises awareness for artists like himself to be part of the mainstream art world. Matthew has made five films that have been shown at film festivals, nationally and internationally.

@matthewhellett

Fights, Rights and Insights

Gavin Harding, MBE

Politics runs in my family. I wanted to follow the family tradition.

My mum's brother was a Labour councillor in Wales and her father loved politics. I used to call him Grampy. My uncle and Grampy had a big impact on me. I used to listen to them discussing the political news, and I'd learn how they used words and how they made their argument. To me, Grampy's front room seemed like the debating chamber in the House of Commons. Grampy used to wind up my uncle deliberately about politics, so they'd have these heated discussions. That's where my interest in politics started.

My uncle tests everyone out. When I was younger, I remember him meeting my cousins' boyfriends or girlfriends and he'd try and figure out their politics. He'd ask what they thought of the Labour Party. If their answer showed they weren't Labour voters, he'd joke, 'There's absolutely no way you're marrying them!'

When my mum married my dad, my uncle got on with my dad because of his politics. Dad was a miner and went out on strike in the 1980s to fight against the colliery closures that were happening then. I remember the public-sector workers striking in the late 1980s, like the nurses, teachers and bus drivers, because the government wanted to cap their pay. The protests inspired me. I was brought up to believe that you take a stand against things you don't agree with.

When I was a boy, it was a time when the Labour Party was more socialist than it is now and you had these big-name Labour politicians like Tony Benn, Michael Foot and Neil Kinnock. They were the people that I looked up to. I heard Michael Foot speak at a gala in Yorkshire when I was really little. My family took me along. I don't remember much about it, but I do know it was a big deal at the time, because he was a famous politician.

I was about eight years old when I made my first political speech. It was about the importance of the NHS. We were visiting the family in Wales and my uncle said I should try speaking from the bedroom window of my uncle's house in Cardiff – like when people give speeches on balconies. I remember Mum walking into the room saying, 'Get back in here now!' I think she thought the neighbours wouldn't like it. She was going mad at my uncle – it was funny. It was only my uncle listening, but it made me think about how to speak in front of people.

*

At secondary school, I was one of the first six pupils in England to use a special educational needs unit in a normal secondary school. The idea of a special unit was new at the time and was brought in by the government so disabled kids would be more integrated. We had a classroom at Brayton High School in Selby and our own teachers, so we had more one-to-one support. We also had some lessons with the other kids in their classrooms.

At first, I didn't want to go to a mainstream school. I'd come from a special school for disabled children and I wasn't sure how I'd fit in. But it was the best thing I could have done, because although I was bullied and made fun of, it made me a stronger person. It made me more determined. Some of the other kids would call me 'spastic' or say I was 'mentally handicapped' – all those awful words. It was daily emotional torture for the first two years until I got more confident.

My confidence came from trying to make people aware of things that I thought were wrong. When I was fourteen or fifteen, I was one of five pupils who fought against the school closing the tuck shop in the common room. The tuck shop was a bit of a treat and it meant we could spend our pocket money on something we wanted. And it gave us something else to do at break times. We went to complain to the head of year. I suppose that was my first experience of lobbying for something I really believed in. Although the school still closed the tuck shop, it was important to challenge something I thought was wrong.

When there was a general election, we had mock elections at school. I stood as one of the Labour candidates and I made a speech. I talked about why politics was important, why people should vote and how government works. I knew this from watching the news and listening to my family talk about politics. I remember feeling fired up by the speech. When I went back to the special needs classroom I wrote 'Vote Labour' across a blackboard to get more people to support me. My teacher rubbed it all out, but I don't remember her being angry. I think she was impressed. She said, 'It wouldn't surprise me if you go into politics.'

I liked school a lot more when I got involved in the school's pupil council. It was my job to represent the views of the special needs kids and make sure that our voice was heard. One issue was that after a couple of years, the school decided to move our classroom to the first floor. But we were worried about the staircase, which used to get crowded and rammed with pupils moving about between lessons. I pointed out our concerns, and the teachers put in a one-way system on the staircase. That was a small victory.

But no one at school asked what I wanted to do with my life. I remember my mum coming back from one parents' evening saying, 'It's going to be very hard for special needs people to get a job.' She'd obviously had words with the teachers about what I'd do when I finished school. The hardest thing was that I wanted to get a job, but I didn't have any qualifications. I also knew there were negative attitudes out there about employing people with learning disabilities, so I just went to college. I did a course in working with children and young people and studied basic skills like maths. I did that for two years, but I wasn't ever sure what it was qualifying me for.

I made a success out of my time at college by joining the student union. I went because I knew it was political, and that's where the action was. By the end of my first year, I was so involved with the union that I became the first person with a learning disability to be its vice president. My tutors told me that students with a learning disability usually just hung around the corridors, and I was doing something different by getting known around the college.

The first thing I did as union vice president was to organise a protest against the college's plan to close down the campus club. To me, it was like the school tuck-shop fight, but bigger. We ran a successful campaign and the club won a reprieve (after I left, the principal demolished it – I think he thought it was safe to bulldoze it once I'd left!). I also protested against government plans to cut grants for mature students and I organised a fundraising concert with college bands in aid of a local homeless hostel. It got headlines in the local paper. The best bit about student politics was that everyone on the union was confident and had a political ego, but we made sure we took action together to represent all the other students.

When I left college I had a period of not knowing what to do. I found myself in a blank space. I did some youth work, both paid and voluntary, but I didn't have a proper job. Having nothing much to do made me anxious and unhappy. The only thing I found at the job centre was a government Youth Training Scheme (YTS) placement working at a stable yard. The YTS gave me on-the-job-training for a year, but there wasn't a guarantee of a job at the end of it. I was hard-working and I learned a lot about horses. I helped with the riding lessons for disabled children, but the stables couldn't take me on after my placement ended.

I found a job working in the stockroom of a high-street shop for four hours a week, then I got a job on the production line of a food factory. It was dull but it did bring in a bit of money. I had a girlfriend but we split up and I went through a bad patch. I sank into a depression and I was drinking too much. My mental health was deteriorating, so I began seeing my local community learning disability team (these teams give specialist health advice to learning-disabled people). It was decided that I needed to be admitted to something called an assessment and treatment unit as an inpatient, to work out what help I needed. I didn't have a name for it then but, looking back, what I went through was a breakdown.

Most people have never heard of assessment and treatment units. They're hospital-style places that are meant to give short-term care to learning-disabled people who are in a crisis. They're for people who have complex needs, like a mental health issue as well as a learning disability. The idea is that you stay there for a few weeks or months to get the help you need. But these places are known for keeping people in too long, many years in some cases. People often get sent to a unit miles away from their home and family and their 'care' involves being restrained by staff, being sedated with strong medication and being kept under lock and key. It's a shocking, outdated system.

Something people will have probably heard of is Winterbourne View. This was an assessment and treatment unit in South Gloucestershire. In 2011, BBC's *Panorama* showed horrific undercover film of patients there being abused by staff. No one was shown any dignity or respect. After that, the government said it would close down units like this and move the thousands of people who were in them back into their own communities, but it's taking a long time. What's awful is that it takes a scandal like Winterbourne View to make people see what's been happening for so long.

I probably spent a total of ten years moving in and out of different units, mostly in the north of England. It was like I was just being passed around the system.

The first place I was in during my early twenties was a couple of hours away from Selby, and I was there for almost two years. It was an unwelcoming place where staff treated people like children. We had to be up and washed by 7 a.m. then have breakfast by 8 a.m. and we were told to go to bed by 9 p.m. It was run by a manager who made us do hospital-corner beds.[1] If you didn't do it right, she and her staff stripped the bed and made you do it again. This was the type of place where if you refused to have what was on the menu, you had a glass of water placed in front of you instead.

The longest time I spent in any unit was over two years, and I missed my family so much because it was almost three hours from where they lived. Living apart from them was hard. People just don't realise the mental torture caused by being separated from your family like that.

For most of my time in the units, I was detained under a particular section of the Mental Health Act (this is what some people call being 'sectioned'), so I could be kept there even if I didn't want to be there. I was put under heavy medication. I was out of it. Staff talked about me like I didn't exist. I felt invisible. How does anyone expect you to get better when you're treated like that?

Before this, I'd never really come across how bad things could be for people with learning disabilities. I felt like up to that point I'd lived a relatively ordinary life. I was shocked, but I did try to stand up to staff and managers when they gave orders to me or the other patients (like telling us to tidy our rooms). I told them not to speak to me or anyone else like that but it didn't make any difference.

I remember a unit manager swearing at someone. When I asked him why he had to use bad language, I got told to mind my own business. I can remember one patient, a man who wasn't able to talk. He refused to eat his dinner and the staff told him to go to his bedroom. We were treated like naughty schoolchildren. I was shocked that people could be treated like this in a place that was meant to support them.

It was bad enough for me in the unit, but at least I could speak up for myself – there were people in these with very complex needs who couldn't even communicate. Imagine how that must feel. It really was like you were being punished all the time. In the hospital, my confidence was knocked back. People hear, but they don't really listen to you in these sorts of places. There was no respect.

There were a few decent people among the staff at the different units I was admitted to, and that's how I got back on track. There was a manager at one place I remember who used to organise staff to take me on days out shopping or to a café. Doing more ordinary things and having my medication reduced helped, and eventually I moved back to Selby. I had my own room in a shared house with care staff visiting to help me with things like keeping appointments or sorting out bills.

The other thing that helped me after I moved home was that I chose to have something called direct payments. This meant that I could arrange my own support directly with a care provider, instead of social services arranging what help I got. It helped me get back control over my life.

I don't think I would have got back into politics and activism without a charity called York People First (YPF). It helped me get back on my feet after the assessment and treatment centres. YPF is an independent group run by people with learning disabilities for people with learning disabilities. I'd heard that YPF did lots of campaigns, so I joined because I wanted to raise awareness about some of the things I'd heard and seen in the assessment and treatment units. The charity's a big part of my success because it helped me rebuild my life and my confidence.

I learned so much at YPF that I started my own local self-advocacy group for people with learning disabilities in Selby, Voices for People. Self-advocacy means you represent yourself, rather than someone who doesn't have a learning disability talking on your behalf.

One of my aims was to get the public to know more about the rights of people with learning disabilities. We ran coffee mornings so learning-disabled people had the chance to talk to each other and evening events like bingo nights. We worked with a local college so people could get qualifications in first aid or food hygiene. This meant they might have a better chance of getting a job.

By this stage, I was getting quite vocal and becoming known around the town, so it felt natural to get involved with the local Labour Party. I went to some local Labour meetings and they asked me to consider standing for the local council ward where I live, Selby Northward. Of course I said yes.

I felt proud to be doing what my uncle had done, and I thought my Grampy would have been so pleased. When I was campaigning for election, I went around knocking on as many doors as I could. Most people who I spoke to told me they never saw the other candidates. But it was important to me to speak to people about what they wanted from their local politician.

It was quite hard on election night, not knowing if I was going to win or not. I wasn't sure, because it was my first election and I didn't know what to expect. But when I saw the votes coming in and I realised I'd won, I remember jumping up in the air. One of the other councillors' wives said, 'That's not really something you should do,' but I couldn't help it. It just felt great.

So in 2011, I became the first person with a learning disability in the UK to be elected as a local councillor.

That's the achievement I'm most proud of in my life so far. Mum was really proud of me, but she joked, 'Oh no, not another politician in the family.' My uncle was really chuffed. When my seat came up for re-election four years later in 2015, I increased my share of the votes from 590 to 1,039.

People who work at the council have learned more about learning disability because of me. Some people might assume I only campaigned about disability, but I didn't. I represented everyone in the area. I remember walking down one street in Selby, and the pavement was in such poor condition, it had obviously been forgotten about. It hadn't had any repairs in the forty years since it was built. I thought how difficult it must be for older people or people with wheelchairs to use it. Repairing that pavement ended up being my first campaign when I was elected, and I got it fixed.

Another one of my campaigns was to get the council to replace the tatty play equipment in two of our local parks. I used to play in them as a kid and I don't think the swings or slides had been changed since then. Some of my other campaigns highlighted how the council needs to attract more shops to the town, and develop more facilities for young people.

Once, I led sixty residents in a campaign to get a pedestrian crossing built on a busy local road. We were told there wasn't any funding, but we made our case and we blocked the road for a few hours in protest. That campaign was made up of all sorts of people: old, young, people with and without disabilities. And we got the crossing.

The other major success in my life is when I became deputy mayor and then mayor of Selby. When it happened, it felt unreal. It was a great honour being mayor of my hometown. I had to chair a lot of council meetings, but being mayor is also a ceremonial role, so I attended local events where I represented the entire council.

While I was mayor, my old secondary school wanted to hold a reunion, so I suggested we have it at the town hall. I wanted to show the bullies how far I'd come, with an event on my turf, the town hall, and as mayor of the whole town.

It was strange coming face to face with some of the people who'd called me names. As mayor, it was my job to greet them. They all shook my hand and acted like none of it had happened. I thought I'd confront them, but I didn't have to say anything because they couldn't even look me in the eye. I thought that was cowardly.

As mayor I attended as many school events as possible, because it's important to educate kids about tolerance towards anyone who's a bit different.

One of my proudest moments was when I was asked to help run a special government project after the Winterbourne View scandal. I felt so angry and upset when I watched the BBC *Panorama* programme that showed the abuse. Although nothing like that had happened to me when I was an inpatient, it brought back memories of an awful time.

The project I helped run was called the Transforming Care Board and it was set up to oversee progress in getting people out of places like Winterbourne View. The Minister for Care and Support at the time, the Liberal Democrat Sir Norman Lamb, asked me to co-chair the board with him. Norman and I put aside our political differences because we had a shared passion about getting people with learning disabilities out of institutions. Norman asked for me as his co-chair because he wanted someone who knew how the institutions worked.

The abuse at Winterbourne View was extreme. But even in places where people with learning disabilities get good care and support, their views might still be ignored. People are sidelined. Too often, the professionals who decide what kind of care people get make these decisions behind closed doors. Things would be so much better if people themselves had a bigger say in their own care, instead of just 'getting treatment' or 'being cared for'. People with learning disabilities have rights and should have choices just like everyone else. It's about listening to what people are saying – or sometimes not saying.

I also helped launch a government consultation paper about how people with learning disabilities, autism and mental health issues are treated by the care system. I helped write the paper *No Voice Unheard, No Right Ignored*. I wrote it because I care about what happens to people with learning disabilities and the effects that places like assessment and treatment units have on people and their families. As someone who has been in these places as a patient, the paper was very close to my heart.

In the consultation paper, I wrote a foreword about what good care looks like. I described how larger units should be closing and how we need small mental health units instead. I also suggested that the health professionals who commission the care should commission more local community providers so people can be helped closer to home. Although the old asylums and long-stay hospitals were meant to have been closed down in the 1980s, we still have these massive places where people's lives are restricted. I don't want people going back into these shocking institutions. Returning home where you grew up is what should be happening.

One thing that worries me is that although there are now fewer people in assessment and treatment units than there were a few years ago, we need to keep this momentum going. I don't want it to be the case that ten years from now, people are still being moved out of their area, miles from their family and friends.

I asked Norman Lamb to write about the time that we spent working together:

I met Gavin Harding early in my time as Minister for Care and Support during the coalition government. This was in the aftermath of the scandal at Winterbourne View. We wanted to establish a board to review and oversee work which the Department of Health was carrying out in the aftermath of Winterbourne View in order to address the fact that so many people continued to live in institutions – long-stay hospitals – even though they were perfectly able to live in the community with support. I invited Gavin to join me in co-chairing the Transforming Care board.

I thought that it was vital to have input from someone with a learning disability – and someone who had experienced what assessment and treatment units were like. Gavin brought that incredible insight. He was brilliant to work with. He was challenging and had strong views but was always willing to discuss issues and to help find solutions. Gavin subsequently worked on the green paper, which was called *No Voice Unheard, No Right Ignored*. His input into that green paper was again invaluable. Civil servants in the department enjoyed working with Gavin.

Gavin was an enormous help to me personally. Before I took on the role of Minister for Care and Support, I did not have in-depth experience of learning disability and so the learning curve for me was very steep. Working with Gavin helped me to understand the key issues. We have a shared passion for ensuring that every citizen is treated as an equal citizen.

There has been a significant wider impact as a result of involving Gavin and others like him at a senior level within government. It forces civil servants and ministers to confront assumptions and sometimes ignorance. It gives insight which otherwise would be lacking. It forces key decision-makers to focus on people and it helps provide a moral imperative to drive change.

And this is an extract from my foreword to the government consultation paper, *No Voice Unheard, No Right Ignored*:

I think it has not mattered who the government was, this has been going on for far too long across several governments: people not having any choice in how they are treated or supported or where they live, people being moved out of their local area to miles away, people being locked away from their families in hospital units, people, in a small minority of places, being abused by staff ... We should not allow scandals like Winterbourne View to be repeated. I, and everyone else with a learning disability, hope to see this end and to start to see everyone with a learning disability or autism or with mental health needs being treated with respect and dignity equal to any other human being. We have the same rights as anyone else. After all, we are not just a label. We are not someone you can treat differently. We are human beings. We have an entitlement to a life just like you. Make the lives of all people with disabilities a good life without barriers.

I became the first person with a learning disability to be employed by the NHS in 2015. I'm a learning disability advisor, and since I began work, two other learning disability advisors have joined my team. We're all on proper wages and have proper jobs and responsibilities. It's important because so few people with a learning disability are in paid work – less than 6 per cent.

I've come a long way since I made that speech as a child about how important the health service is. I still have to pinch myself when I think I've ended up working for the public service I made my first speech about.

My job as a learning disability advisor is to help make

sure that the NHS improves the way it cares for and treats learning-disabled people. It's my responsibility to help make sure that their views are represented in the health system.

One of the important areas I work on is NHS care and treatment reviews. I wish these reviews had been around when I was in an assessment and treatment unit. They mean that if you're in hospital for a mental health problem or what they call 'challenging behaviour' (this can be anything from self-harm to hurting other people), you have a right to a review that can help you get support in the community instead.

When I first began working for the NHS, I think it was a surprise for some colleagues who'd had clinical or nursing jobs in learning disability. They were more used to treating people like me as patients, not as colleagues who are equal. It took them time to get used to the fact that I was challenging them about some of their methods.

I was pointing out things like the fact that job application forms were too complicated, and the NHS needed to produce accessible versions. Some people had to get used to the fact that someone like me was taking the lead on visits to hospitals or at meetings to talk about how to make the NHS better for learning-disabled people. When I started my NHS job, I was asked how best people could support me. I said I needed to be given freedom to express myself, and I needed people to talk to me.

One of the best moments I've had so far in this job was in a meeting about how to make it easier for people to move out of places like Winterbourne View. I was speaking to a group that included staff and patients from assessment and treatment units. Afterwards, one man who was due to leave his unit told me that hearing from an ex-patient like me had inspired him and made him think more positively about his future. That touched me.

Doing this job hasn't always been easy, though. My experience of campaigning is with small charities, so the first few months in a big organisation like the NHS took me a while to actually get into. But I have some really good support from my colleagues in my team, which makes all the difference.

Colleagues who don't have learning disabilities support the three of us learning disability advisors. Steve Mbara was my learning disability support officer when I started the job and he really helped me. I need help with things like emails, planning events and handling my diary. I have the vision, but the support I get helps with the practical steps to make things happen.

I count Steve and Maggie Graham, another colleague without a learning disability, as friends too. I speak to them if I've got worries, whether that's to do with work or something more personal. If it wasn't for the team I'm working with, I don't think I could do my job. People see me as a person who has achieved things, but it doesn't mean I don't have problems or I don't need support. The key thing is the people I've got around me in my team.

I feel proud that I work for a national industry like the NHS and that it's employing people with learning disabilities. My growing commitments with my NHS role meant I had to stand down from the council in 2019. I know some people with learning disabilities might think I've sold out because I'm no longer campaigning, but I want to change the system from the inside. I'm still doing what I've always done, it's just that I'm doing it from the other side of the fence. Our office feels like the headquarters of a learning disability campaign group within the NHS because of the way we work to influence people.

At work I'm an analytical thinker and a savvy negotiator. People admire my creative ideas and my willingness to learn and understand new things. If there's a problem, I want to help fix it. The most important thing to me, apart from my family and friends, is that I'm able to influence and change things. I'm driven by a desire to change people's lives, especially people who are in the position I was in when I spent time in the units.

One of my strongest skills is that I'm able to speak up for myself and for other people. I'll fight for people's rights, so if I think something's wrong I'll want to do something about it. I'm honest and I'm quite practical. An example of this that still makes my family laugh is when I was best man at my best friend's wedding, and at the wedding rehearsal the vicar asked if anyone had any questions. I asked where the fire doors were. My friend just looked at me. I have a dry sense of humour too.

Having social skills is a really important part of working. A lot of people get a job but aren't taught how to get along in the workplace. It's important to know how to have banter – the water-cooler conversations – and how to challenge someone's decision without getting angry. I'm into football (I support Hull City), so that can be an icebreaker if there's nothing else to chat about. I also read a lot of autobiographies. I've read Tony Blair's and the autobiography by the actor and political activist Ricky Tomlinson, who played Jim Royle in *The Royle Family*. I'm a confident public speaker too and not just at work. I did the best man's speech at my brother's wedding too.

I have a busy life outside work. I've got three nephews and a niece, and I'm honoured to have three godchildren. I take my job as godfather seriously; it's a responsibility and I'm privileged to be trusted to take on the role. If I've got time off, I also like going to the Yorkshire Dales – it's beautiful up there. Something that surprises a lot of people is that I'm really into my music. I'm a child of the eighties, so I love eighties pop music, like Deacon Blue. I also listen to a lot of American rap, house and garage music. I listen to it at home or on my headphones on my way into work. It keeps me calm and puts me in a good mood.

The biggest problems for people with learning disabilities today are the changes to the benefit system and the impact this has on people being able to live their lives.

Cuts to people's support makes it harder for them to live independently, and I worry if this means they might have to go and live in an institution just to get the support they need to live (I have a carer who helps me keep on top of things like my washing and housework for three hours a week).

I felt so strongly about the government cuts to disabled people's support that I almost didn't accept my MBE. But my family persuaded me to accept it on behalf of people with learning disabilities, to show what we can do.

My MBE, and my work in politics and in the NHS, shows that learning-disabled people can achieve things that people think are unachievable. There's nothing that should be impossible. If it's possible for me to be a mayor, then other people can do it too. It's just about getting the right support – and for me it was also about getting involved in local campaigning and learning to speak up for myself. It's about growing your confidence.

I want to make sure there are more people going into politics. So I'd say to young people, get into politics, join your local party. Get involved, get yourself known and don't forget you're fighting for everyone's issues – whether it's about families in poverty, tenancy issues, dog muck on the pavements, or even the tuck shop at school. The people have elected you in, so you're there to fight their corner. You need to stand up for yourself and for other people.

Something that's helped me in my local government and my NHS career is that I've listened to other, more experienced colleagues. I listen to other people and I learn from them. I've also been successful in local government because I don't just represent people with learning disabilities. Trying to act on behalf of everyone has made my eyes open wider, although part of my work is also to open other people's eyes to issues they might not have thought of before, like how badly some people with learning disabilities are treated.

I've broken barriers, and I'm proud of what I've done, but the most important thing is that what I've done inspires other people.

I was the first councillor with learning disabilities and then the first mayor.

I was the first, and I shouldn't be the last.

Gavin Harding became the first learning-disabled person to be elected on to a local council when he became a Labour councillor in his hometown of Selby, Yorkshire, in 2011. In 2015 he became the UK's first mayor with learning disabilities and the first person with a learning disability to be employed by NHS England, where he works as a learning disability advisor. His work with government includes helping draw up a three-year plan on learning disability, Valuing People Now, in 2009. He co-chaired a group to improve standards of care for people with learning disabilities, the Transforming Care programme, in 2014. Gavin was awarded an MBE for services to people with learning disabilities in 2014. In 2019 he helped produce *Beyond the high fence* for NHS England, a report about seeing what is possible for people who have been in prison, hospital or both. He is an ardent opponent of institutional care after mental health difficulties in his early twenties led him to spend several years in a series of secure hospital units.

@gavhardingmbe

Notes

Untold Success

1   A learning disability affects intellectual ability. It impacts on how someone
    understands information and communications, and affects their ability to do everyday
    tasks independently. A learning difficulty (like dyslexia) is different because it does
    not impact on intellectual development. Autism is not a learning disability, nor is the
    physical disability cerebral palsy – although people with these conditions might also
    have a learning disability. A learning disability is not a mental health issue – although
    a learning-disabled person might also have a mental health issue.

2   It is for this reason that some of the essayists describe or define their learning disability
    (referring to an official 'diagnosis', for example, if they have one) while others do not.

3   Richard Adams, 'Special needs funding at crisis point, say school leaders', *Guardian*,
    5 September 2018, https://www.theguardian.com/education/2018/sep/05/special-
    needs-funding-at-crisis-point-say-school-leaders

4   *Stuck at home: the impact of day service cuts on people with a learning disability*, Mencap,
    London, 2012, p. 2.

5   Ibid., p. 5.

6   Dr Simon Duffy, *A fair society? How the cuts target disabled people*, Centre for Welfare
    Reform, London, 2013, p. 7.

7   *Inquiry concerning the United Kingdom of Great Britain and Northern Ireland carried
    out by the Committee under article 6 of the Optional Protocol to the Convention*, United
    Nations, Geneva, 2016, p. 20.

8   '*Being disabled in Britain: a journey less equal*', Equality and Human Rights
    Commission, London, 2017, p. 5.

9   'About Fragile X Syndrome', The Fragile X Society, http://www.fragilex.org.uk/
    syndrome

10 Sally Weale and Niamh McIntyre, 'Special needs pupils being failed by system
    "on verge of crisis"', *Guardian*, 22 October 2018, https://www.theguardian.com/
    education/2018/oct/22/special-needs-pupils-being-failed-by-system-on-verge-crisis

11 Founded in 1939 in Aberdeen, the Camphill Movement started with a single school, and expanded to over a hundred schools and communities worldwide. The communities are all individual entities but share a similar approach, which is to value the 'profound significance of each human being'. The aim is to enable and encourage learning-disabled people to develop a sense of belonging and purpose.

12 David Brindle, 'How actor Brian Rix has been putting learning disabilities centre stage', *Guardian,* 22 January 2014, https://www.theguardian.com/society/2014/jan/22/brian-rix-actor-learning-disabilities-mencap

13 Suzannah Lipscomb, 'All the King's Fools', History Today, 8 August 2011, https://www.historytoday.com/suzannah-lipscomb/all-king%E2%80%99s-fools

14 'Social history of learning disability', Langdon Down Museum, https://langdondownmuseum.org.uk/the-history-of-learning-disability/social-history-of-learning-disability/

15 Andy Merriman, *Tales of Normansfield: The Langdon Down Legacy*, Down's Syndrome Association, Middlesex, 2007, p. 39.

16 The Grade II listed theatre still hosts events and is managed by charity the Down's Syndrome Association, which is based at Normansfield and runs the Langdon Down Museum of Learning Disability.

17 Andy Merriman, *Tales of Normansfield*, p. 28.

18 'Disabled People', Holocaust Memorial Trust, https://www.hmd.org.uk/learn-about-the-holocaust-and-genocides/nazi-persecution/disabled-people/

19 '"Mental Deficiency" between the Wars – Life in the Colony', Historic England, https://historicengland.org.uk/research/inclusive-heritage/disability-history/1914-1945/mental-deficiency-between-the-wars/

20 'Mabel Cooper's life story', Open University Social History of Learning Disability, http://www.open.ac.uk/health-and-social-care/research/shld/resources-and-publications/life-stories/mabels-story/part-1-life-story/hospital. This research led to a subsequent book: Dorothy Atkinson, Mark Jackson, Jan Walmsley (eds), *Forgotten Lives: Exploring the History of Learning Disability*, British Institute of Learning Disabilities, Kidderminster, 1997.

21 Geoffrey Howe, *Report of the Committee of Inquiry into allegations of ill-treatment of patients and other irregularities at the Ely Hospital, Cardiff*, HMSO, 1969.

22 *Silent Minority* (1981), Nigel Evans, https://www.bfi.org.uk/films-tv-people/4ce2b69b6c084

23 *Report of the Committee of Inquiry into Normansfield Hospital*, Department of Health and Social Security, HMSO, 1978.

24 *Better Services for the Mentally Handicapped*, Department of Health and Social Security, HMSO, 1971.

25 Quoted in Merriman, *Normansfield*, p. 9.

26 Mark Brend, *First and Last – Closing Learning Disabilities Hospitals*, Choice Support, London, 2008, pp. 11–12.

NOTES

27 *Valuing People: A New Strategy for Learning Disability for the 21st Century*, Department of Health, HMSO, London, 2001.

28 Margaret Flynn, *Winterbourne View Hospital: A Serious Case Review*, South Gloucestershire Safeguarding Adults Board, South Gloucestershire Council, 2012, p. 122.

29 The definition of 'challenging behaviour' as outlined by Professor Jim Mansell. *Services for people with learning disabilities and challenging behaviour or mental health needs (*aka the *Mansell Report*), Department of Health, 2007.

30 *Transforming Care: A national response to Winterbourne View Hospital*, Department of Health, HMSO, London, 2012, p. 9.

31 'Learning Disability Services Monthly Statistics', NHS Digital, https://digital.nhs.uk/data-and-information/publications/statistical/learning-disability-services-statistics/at-october-2019-mhsds-august-2019-final

32 Saba Salman, 'Charity helpline supports abuse victims with learning disabilities', *Guardian*, 7 May 2014, https://www.theguardian.com/social-care-network/2014/may/07/charity-helpline-abuse-victims-learning-disability

33 Steven Morris, 'Care home directors convicted over "horrific" learning disability regime', *Guardian*, 7 June 2017, https://www.theguardian.com/society/2017/jun/07/care-home-directors-convicted-over-devon-learning-disability-regime *Ibid.* 'Somerset care home staff bullied autistic residents, review finds', 8 February 2018, https://www.theguardian.com/society/2018/feb/08/somerset-care-home-staff-bullied-autistic-residents-review-finds

34 Saba Salman, 'You can't rehabilitate someone into society when they're locked away', *Guardian*, 16 January 2019, https://www.theguardian.com/society/2019/jan/16/rehab-centre-learning-disabilities-secure-units-community

35 *The state of care in mental health services 2014–2017*, Care Quality Commission, London, 2017, p. 5.

36 Ian Birrell, 'A teen with autism is locked in solitary confinement and being fed through a hatch. Have we really moved on from Bedlam?', iNews, 7 October 2018, https://inews.co.uk/opinion/nhs-treatment-learning-difficulties-bedlam/

37 'Stopping over medication of people with a learning disability, autism or both (STOMP)', NHS England, https://www.england.nhs.uk/learning-disabilities/improving-health/stomp/

38 Lucy Adams, '"Shameful" use of restraints on disabled patients', BBC News, 2 October 2018, https://www.bbc.co.uk/news/uk-45652339

39 'Almost 1 in 3 young people with a learning disability spend less than an hour a day outside homes – survey of 18–35-year-olds with a learning disability', Mencap, 19 January 2016, https://www.mencap.org.uk/press-release/almost-1-3-young-people-learning-disability-spend-less-hour-day-outside-homes-survey

40 Elaine James, Mark Harvey, Rob Mitchell, *An Inquiry by Social Workers into Evening Routines in Community Living Settings for Adults with Learning Disabilities*, Lancaster University, 2017.

41 *The Learning Disabilities Mortality Review*, Bristol University commissioned by the Healthcare Quality Improvement Partnership on behalf of NHS England, May 2018.

42 Paula McGowan, 'Prevent avoidable deaths by making autism/learning disability training mandatory', UK Government and Parliament Petitions, 2018, https://petition.parliament.uk/petitions/221033

43 Monica McCaffrey, 'Siblings of disabled people know them best. Let's use their insight', *Guardian*, 7 August 2018, https://www.theguardian.com/society/2018/aug/07/siblings-disabled-people-care-providers-family-charity

44 Sara Ryan, 'Imagined futures', mydaftlife, 19 April 2014, https://mydaftlife.com/2014/04/19/imagined-futures/

45 Sara Ryan, *Justice for Laughing Boy*, Jessica Kingsley Publishers, London, 2018.

46 'Just 30% of public say they would feel comfortable sitting next to a person with a learning disability, survey finds', *Learning Disability Today*, 21 October 2016, https://www.learningdisabilitytoday.co.uk/just-30-of-public-say-they-would-feel-comfortable-sitting-next-to-a-person-with-a-learning-disability-survey-finds

47 'Say NO more autism and learning disability hate crime', Dimensions, https://www.dimensions-uk.org/get-involved/campaigns/say-no-autism-learning-disability-hate-crime-imwithsam/

48 Chris Hatton, 'Employment statistics – quick update', https://chrishatton.blogspot.com/2017/11/employment-statistics-quick-update.html

49 Eric Emerson, Sally Malam, Ian Davies and Karen Spencer, *Adults with Learning Difficulties in England 2003–4*, Health and Social Care Information Centre, 2005, p. 4.

50 Frances Ryan, 'Looking for work with a learning disability: "You feel like a failure"', *Guardian*, https://www.theguardian.com/careers/2017/may/08/looking-for-work-with-a-learning-disability-you-feel-like-a-failure

51 'Whilst the initiatives are not all aimed exclusively at people with a learning difficulty or disability, we expect that many will benefit from them', quoted in briefing paper *Learning disability policy and services*, House of Commons Library, 18 September 2018, p. 17.

52 Saba Salman, 'Cutting employment support for learning-disabled people is a false economy', *Guardian*, 5 May 2015, https://www.theguardian.com/society/2015/may/05/learning-disability-employment-support-cut-false-economy-benefits

53 'So, who exactly can be supported into employment?', Dimensions, November 2015, https://www.dimensions-uk.org/best-practice-post/exactly-can-supported-employment/

54 'The nature of entrepreneurship and enterprise for people with learning disabilities', Mutually Inclusive, http://www.mutuallyinclusive.co.uk/research.html

55 *Valuing employment now: Real jobs for people with learning disabilities*, Department of Health, London, 2009.

56 Jim Mansell, *Raising our sights: Services for adults with profound intellectual and multiple learning disabilities*, Department of Health, London, 2010.

57 'Who will care after I'm gone?', FitzRoy, Hampshire, 2015, https://www.fitzroy.org/wp-content/uploads/Who-will-care-after-im-gone.pdf

58 While the NHS Long Term Plan published in 2019 included commitments to improve learning disability nationally, these have been criticised for lacking in ambition and for repeating previously published targets. 'The NHS 10 year – what we are thinking so far', 9 January 2019, Learning Disability England, http://www.learningdisabilityengland.org.uk/news/the-nhs-10-year-what-we-are-thinking-so-far/

59 Rob Greig, 'The case for a new "Valuing People" (but not called that)', NDTi, 18 September 2018, https://www.ndti.org.uk/blog/the-case-for-a-new-valuing-people-but-not-called-that

Champagne, Snakes and Stealing Chips

1 'Diversity at the Oscars', Mencap, 26 February 2017, https://www.mencap.org.uk/press-release/diversity-oscars-disabled-actors-and-organisations-publish-letter-calling-more

Fights, Rights and Insights

1 Doing 'hospital corners' refers to a way of making a bed with neat, overlapping folds that secure the sheet tightly under the mattress.

Editor's Acknowledgements

At the heart of *Made Possible* is the idea that with the right support you can achieve your goals, so I need to thank the many people who helped to get this book published.

This book would never have seen the light of day without the individuals and organisations that backed it; my sincere thanks to everyone who crowdfunded *Made Possible* or helped spread word about it. A massive thank you to all the fantastic contributors and their families, friends, colleagues and support staff. Shaun, Sarah, Gary, Lizzie, Dan, Laura, Matthew, Gavin – you've made working on this book an absolute joy and a privilege. Particular thanks to Jane, Jere and Cat Gordy, Esther Broughton, Lizzie Banks, Steve Mbara, Philipa Bragman, Bridget Pike and Sandra Reynolds. Thanks also to everyone I've worked with at Unbound, in particular Jimmy Leach, Georgia Odd, Becca Harper-Day, Mark Bowsher and DeAndra Lupu.

Several people shared their time and insights, which were invaluable in shaping this book, so thank you to Michael

Edwards, Pam Bebbington, Paul Scarrott, Sara Ryan, Mark Brookes, Katherine Runswick-Cole, Dan Goodley, John Hersov, Steve Scown, Jackie Fletcher, Ian Jones-Healey, Sir Norman Lamb and the Langdon Down Museum of Learning Disability.

I'm also indebted to Vicki Donlevy, Mary O'Hara, Rob Greig, Rhidian Hughes and David Brindle for much-needed advice and opinions. And a very big thank you to Mark Brend for believing this book would happen in the first place and for being its earliest, most indispensible cheerleader.

Thanks also to Alison Benjamin and Clare Horton at the *Guardian* for the encouragement and supporting the kind of articles that helped influence *Made Possible*. I'm also grateful to Gillian Darley and Nikki Dupin for letting me pick their brains about books, and to Nicola Bensley for her vital, creative perspective.

I have to give a special mention to my parents, Meher and Asad, and my younger sister, Abi, for the support and for allowing me to share our family's experiences. Thanks also to Caroline Gould who, along with Meher, provided practical (i.e. child-related) backup while this book was underway.

My love and thanks to Rob, Maya and Sami Gould, who lived with the idea for this project for a good while before it came to fruition. Rob, your support and encouragement (along with your unofficial role as in-house editorial consultant) made this book's journey from first spark to eventual publication so much smoother than it would have been otherwise.

EDITOR'S ACKNOWLEDGEMENTS

And, of course, I reserve the biggest mention for my youngest sister Raana for sharing her story and, in doing so, showing us all what can be *Made Possible*.

Thanks, Raans – you're pucking brilliant.

Unbound is the world's first crowdfunding publisher, established in 2011.

We believe that wonderful things can happen when you clear a path for people who share a passion. That's why we've built a platform that brings together readers and authors to crowdfund books they believe in – and give fresh ideas that don't fit the traditional mould the chance they deserve.

This book is in your hands because readers made it possible. Everyone who pledged their support is listed below. Join them by visiting unbound.com and supporting a book today.

With grateful thanks to Dimensions for its generous support of this book.

With thanks also to the special supporters of this book:
Simon Berry
John and Judy Bull
Certitude
Robert, Maya and Sami Gould
Abi, Ehsan and Zaki Haque
My Life My Choice
Nayyar Naqvi
Royal Mencap Society
Meher and Asad Salman
United Response

John Adams
Aerende (Emily Mathieson)
Helen Ainsworth
Sharon Allen
Debbie Andalo
Alison Anderson
Mark Appleton
Cindy-Jane Armbruster
Richard Ashcroft
Casey Atkinson
Becky Baldwin
Katie Barnett
Saskia Baron
Sarah Bartlett
Ben, Ruth, Iris + Zoe
Alison Benjamin
Nicola Bensley
Clare Bentley
Lady Best-Shaw
Jude Bissett
Emma Blount
Claire Bonniol
Polly Bowler
Philipa Bragman
Brazen Productions
Stuart Brett
David Brindle
Kevin Brinkhurst
Catherine Brown

Hayley Butcher
Lois Cameron
Claire Camplin
Angie Carter
Katie Cebula
Wing-she Chan
Kashaf Chaudhry
Sue Chesworth
Denise Chevin
Paul Child
Jane Chong
Sam Clark
Adam Cobham
Alex Cobham
Philippa Cochrane
Nadia Cohen
Christopher Collingridge
Anthony Comber-Badu
Companions from Hillcrest at
    Lantern Community uk
James Cook
Karen Cooper
Liz Corkhill
Alison Cowen
Martin Coyle
Andrew Cozens
John Crawford
Tamsin Daniel
Gillian Darley

SUPPORTERS

Lander & Daisy Davidson

Melanie Davies

Francine de Stoppelaar

Jess Donlevy

Michael Donlevy

Vicki Donlevy

Oliver Downing

Aisling Duffy

Nikki Dupin

Susan Ebbels

Lou Edward

Shanti Edwards

Angela Ellis

Ruth Evans

Simon Everest

Charles Fernyhough

Roger Fielding

Christine Fletcher

David Floyd

Annah Foden

Charlotte Forwood

Alex Fox

Ben Furner

Nicole Geerkens

Maggie Giddings

Jackie Goldstraw

Jorge Gomes Parein

Mik Goodram

Catherine Gordon

Caroline Gould

Will & Zoe Gould

Sheree Green

Rob Greig

Penelope-Anne Hadley

Matt Hall

Karen Halvey

Zaki Haque

Steven Hardy

Raisa Hassan

Teresa Hassell

Chris Hatton

Carolyn Hawkins

Fran Healey

Tony Heaton OBE

Graham Henderson

Emma Herbert

Kerry Herbert

Ryan Herman

Sian Herschel

Sally Hilton

Elaine Hindle

Robert Holland

Sheila Hollins

Annie Holmes

Tiffany Homsi

Lisa Hopkins

Jackie Howes

David Hughes

Rhidian Hughes

Sze, Pete & Noah Hunter

Lucy Hurst-Brown

Lizzie Huxley-Jones

Stephanie Isaacs

Jermaine Ivey

Eve Jackson

Romana Jafri

Tom and Claire Jaggers

George Julian

Cathy Kafka

Anne Kavanagh

Majid Kazmi

Andrew Kells

Sarah Kidner

Dan Kieran

Joey Latham

Taryl Law

Diane Lightfoot

Beckie Lisney

Adam Long

James Long

Bill Love

Emma Luckhurst

Gaye Lynn

Thessa Mac

Stuart Macdonald

Cader MacPhail

Sarah Maguire

Kamran Mallick

Alexandre Mars

Daniel Marsden

June Marshall

Mandy Marshall

Vanessa Marshall

Briony Martin

Mano Mason

Sarah Mawby

Bernie Mayall

Anna Mayer

Peter Maynard

Carol McBride

Monica McCaffrey

Michelle McCarthy

Deborah McCormick-Guest

Deborah McManamon

Andy McNicoll

Ed Melia

Pen Mendonca

Ali Mercer

Julie Meredith

Andrew Merriman

Graham Miles

Milestones Trust

John Mitchinson

Kamin Mohammadi

The Moles

Abi Monk

SUPPORTERS

Krista Montgomery

Hannah Morgan

Susanne Morris

Bill Mumford

Anna Murphy

Hazel Nancarrow

Amir Naqvi

Arif Naqvi

Hilary and Asghar Naqvi

Misbah Naqvi

Carlo Navato

Antony Nelson

Zophia Newborne

Julie Newcombe

Hayley Newman

Lasse Nielsen

John O'Brien

Mary O'Hara

Niall O'Kane

Jane O'Sullivan

Sally Pacy

Jeff Parry

Ashita Patel

Sophie Paterson

Georgia Pavlopoulou

Adam Pepper

Penny Pepper

Kevin Peter Murphy

Susi Petherick

Richard Phoenix

Jill Pluquailec

Justin Pollard

Amir Porat

Jackie Potter

Mandy Pursey

Cara Quinn Larkin

Aamna Raza

Tiffany Reading

Justin Rehal

Paul Richards

Jane Richardson

Lisa Richardson

Helen Ries

Barbie RNLD

Lucy Rogers (@DrLucyRogers)

Alan Rosenbach

Guido Rößling

Rebecca Rumsey

Katherine Runswick-Cole

Jonathan Ruppin

Sara Ryan

Emma Salman

Raana Salman

Saba Salman

Zahid Salman

Ranjit Sanghera

Tim Saxton

Jane Schaffer

Jenny Schwarz

SeeAbility

Jonathan Senker

Ben Serbutt

Jennifer Shairp

Sarah Shannon

Emmeline Sharp

Tayyauba Sheikh

Elizabeth Shepherd

John Shirlaw

Faizan Shoaib

Jane Sinclair

Kuljit Singh

Sam Sly

Geraint Smith

Jackie Smith

Laura Smith

Maria Stalbow

Alison and Anne Stewart

Marsh Stitchman

Alison Stradling

John Sturgis

Jan Sunman

Kirsty Syder

Annalise Taylor

Louie Thomas

Annie Tidbury

John Tizard

Kate Tokley

Ellen Tomlinson

Liam Toner

Brigitte van Rooij

Claudia Wakefield

Jenny Walker

Sally Warren

John Wearing

Richard West

Hannah Whelan

Margaret White

Kate Whittaker

Will Wiles

Jen Williams

Mark Williams

Catherine Williamson

Alicia Wood

B Woodley

Annabel Wright

Zainub Zainub

Lynne Zwink